The Wedding Photo

The Wedding Photo

DAN A. OREN

RIMMON PRESS

FIRST EDITION: July 2018

Oren, Dan A., 1958–

The Wedding Photo / Dan A. Oren

ISBN: 978-0-692-13981-3

Book design by Meghan Day Healey of Story Horse, LLC

For Sarah, Amalyah, Liam,
and any children of the future

჈

Contents

Introduction

$\mathcal{S}$hakespeare's Juliet Capulet asks, "What's in a name?" Mature adults have learned to answer this question in the same way that Juliet does, "That which we call a rose, [by] any other name would smell as sweet."[1] In other words, what we are called is not what makes us who we are. How we are is who we are. And yet, perhaps Juliet's unforgettable reply is far too simple for the human condition. For me, certainly, it is part of who I am. My name is Dan Ahiassaf Oren. I was born Dan Ahiassaf in Milwaukee, Wisconsin in 1958. From that change of names, made by my parents when I was but age two, and from changes made long before that, my interest in names and history surely begins. My paternal grandfather, born Shmuel Beyrak in Vilna (Vilnius, Lithuania) in 1902 had been left orphaned at age fourteen by a typhus epidemic during the German occupation of the area in World War I. Finding a new direction, in 1921 he left Vilnius to make his adult life in Palestine. There, he followed a common practice and exchanged his European surname for "Ahiassaf," a Hebraicized version of "my brother Josef." He took the Ahiassaf name in memory of his brother Josef, a Russian soldier in the Czar's army who had been killed in the 1914 Battle of Galicia between Russia and Austro-Hungary. A generation later, for economic opportunity and because it was easier to live an ocean away from my difficult paternal grandmother, my parents left Israel for the US, where I was born. In the US their Ahiassaf surname was unusual and, more problematic, unpronounceable for the American tongue. Therefore, my immigrant parents made Ahiassaf our common middle name and added "Oren" as our surname. Oren—a generic name they liked—was easy to say and as recognizable in English as it was in Hebrew. Retaining Ahiassaf, however, they did not erase our past. For that reason, from the first moments I considered my middle and last names, therefore, Juliet's answer to her rhetorical question was never enough. I knew that a name could tell a story.

During my 1960s childhood, an era when international travel was expensive and exotic, I had very limited in-person contact with both sets of grandparents who remained in Israel. I still vividly remember, however, my family's visiting Israel when I was age nine. While there we took a "field trip" with my grandfather Shmuel Ahiassaf to visit the Tel Aviv Police Department, where he served as a beloved chief inspector. I specifically recall the crime scene reconstruction room, where he and his colleagues built dioramas depicting the offenses under investigation. He showed us the interrogation rooms where a suspect could be interviewed while being watched by others through a one-way mirror. Though my own childhood was not traumatized along the lines of Orson Welles's mythical Charles Foster Kane, perhaps in the way that "Citizen Kane" kept his "Rosebud" sled throughout his life, with relatively few talismans to connect me to my grandparents, five decades later I still treasure the two by three inch piece of one-way glass that my grandfather gave me that day as a souvenir. Similarly, a Tel Aviv day trip that same month in Israel with my maternal grandfather Avraham Tzvi Majzels led him to take me out and offer me any souvenir I wanted to buy. I ended up choosing a small hand-cranked pencil sharpener that looked like a globe. It would have been an odd choice for most kids, but that was what I wanted that day. Though I rarely use pencils anymore, and long ago switched to using an electrical pencil sharpener, I still treasure the sharpener my grandfather bought me. A piece of glass and a child's utensil are as valuable to me as any other possession I own.

I did not follow a police detective career as one grandfather had. My other grandfather worked as an administrative clerk and published local history as an amateur. And I did not choose a career as an administrator or a historian. Looking back, however, I can imagine my interest in uncovering genealogical history as flowing in some way from both my grandparents. I can't say specifically whether I inherited genes that might make one a detective and a historian, or whether the environmental influence they passed on to my parents would echo in the work I would do described in this book. But I can't discount these influences that would emerge a decade later in college.

In the fall of 1976, I was a young sophomore at Yale College. It was the two hundreth anniversary year of the United States of America as a nation, and its bicentennial was being celebrated throughout the country. That fall, the Department of Religious Studies at Yale offered a course in American Jewish History. Lloyd Gartner, a visiting professor from the Jewish Theological Seminary in New York and Tel Aviv University in Israel, had been hired for the semester to travel from New York up to

New Haven one day each week for the course. The course consisted of one weekly lecture and discussion session with Professor Gartner and outside readings he assigned. The entire grade for the class was to be based on a term paper on any subject of our choice in American Jewish History, with the proviso that it had to be based in large part on primary source documents. It would not suffice for us to read others' work and then integrate it. We had to get our hands dirty in the way that graduate students and professors do research and examine the original unfiltered documents and records that form history.

As part of my term paper surveying the history of Jews at Yale, I decided I would try to identify who were the first Jewish students to have attended Yale after its founding in 1701. Following on the work of others who had previously pondered this esoteric question, I found myself investigating the genealogy of the Pinto family of the New Haven, Connecticut area. The Pintos, typical of the earliest known Jewish settlers in the American colonies, were of Sephardic Jewish ancestry. And typical of their compatriots, they soon were intermarrying with non-Jews. The question at hand for me was whether the first Pintos to attend Yale were Jewish or not, both in terms of ethnic background and in terms of identity. As I was poring over their genealogical records, to the extent I could find them, I had a moment of insight. I realized at that point that I knew a lot more about this otherwise obscure 300-year-old Pinto family and their history than I knew about my own. Something was wrong with that picture. My encounter with the Pintos spurred me to want to know about my own family's story.

In my case, my unawareness of family history was not caused only by the distance that physically had separated me from my birth and childhood in the US and my grandparents in Israel and the stories they might have told. The other cause was the *Shoah*, and its impact on world Jewry.

Shoah literally means catastrophe, and I shall largely use that term in this book rather than the more popular term of "Holocaust" because the latter implies a holy sacrificial offering that adds a sacredness to a human work of pure evil. To a large degree, the terrible disaster that especially befell European Jewry in the mid-twentieth century reverberated in the minds of Israeli Jews. In addition to the *Shoah* representing an unprecedented and terrible loss of life, for many Israeli Jews the disaster for European Jewry represented a failure of a past way of life. Often, as in my family then, the stories of pre-war Europe failed to be passed down in oral family communication, even if they were recorded in books and museums.

So began my slow process of asking my parents about my own family history, which led to me asking other relatives, which led me to my hobby of studying genealogy. What I quickly found was that much of it could be as exciting as a Sherlock Holmes mystery. Previously unknown and unimagined family members lurked behind names, photos, and files. Shedding light on hidden narratives fueled a fire of excitement that kept burning.

Perhaps my first genealogical exploration was about 1990 when I joined the Jewish Genealogical Society of Greater Washington, DC and found a copy of the "Jewish Genealogical Family Finder." What had started in 1982 as a thirty-seven page typewritten roster of ancestral homes and surnames being researched by members of the New York-based Jewish Genealogical Society had been computerized by genealogist Gary Mokotoff into a world-wide resource whereby massive printouts listing an ever-growing list of surnames, towns, and researchers were distributed worldwide twice a year. I decided I would cast a few crumbs of information into the waters of genealogy and search for information about my father's mother's family of origin: the Schweitzers of Vilna. I had known my grandmother's mother (born Sarah Schweitzer) as she

My grandmother with her sister, mother,
grandmother, and great-grandmother

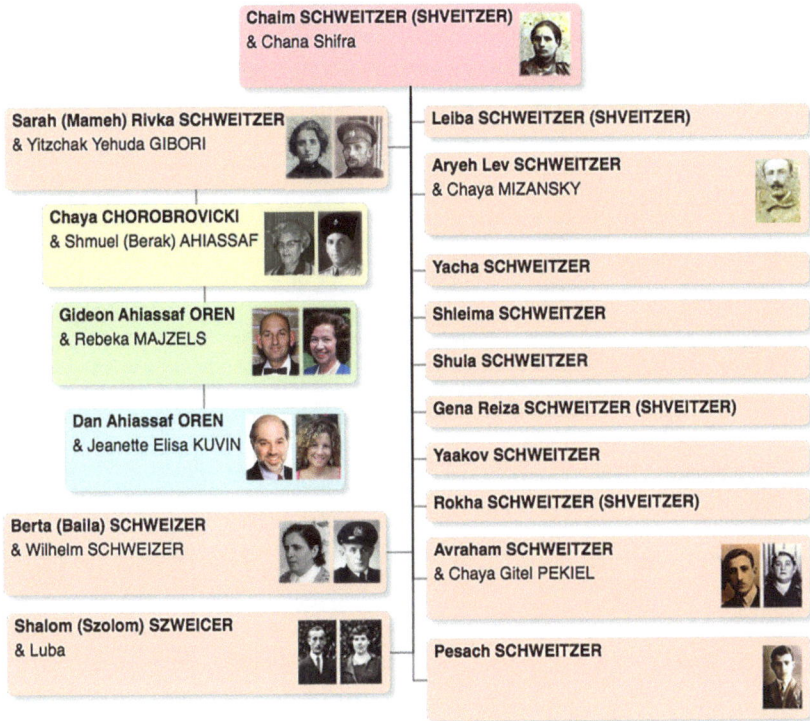

Schweitzer family tree

had lived to a fulsome age, reaching ninety-six in 1982 in Israel. I was in possession of an extraordinary multi-generation photo from about 1909 showing my grandmother (the child in the dark dress), her sibling, my great-grandmother, my great-great-grandmother, and my great-great-great-grandmother—looking as dour as one could be.

My great-grandmother Sarah was one of about a dozen siblings whose ancestry and progeny were essentially unknown to me. I could trace my paternal ancestry via my father to my grandmother Chaya (the girl standing in the photo) and my great-grandmother Sarah Schweitzer (whom everyone called "Mameh"). Old relatives told me the names of her siblings and, with a few photos, I could assemble the family tree above.

All the Schweitzer family that I knew of were connected with Israel. I entered the name of Schweitzer from Vilna into the massive paper-viewed Jewish Genealogical Family Finder database. This action soon slipped away from my personal radar screen. About four years later, a nearly forty-year-old Brooklyn-born man named Samuel Schweitzer attended a primer course on Jewish genealogy at New York University. He found a copy of the Family Finder and noticed that I had submitted a query about Schweitzers from the same town where he knew his father's family had hailed from before the Second World War. Soon enough, he found my telephone number in Maryland and called me one evening. He told me of his father Harry (aka Chaim) Schweitzer, who had been born in Belarus into a big Schweitzer family and who had survived the war with his sister and mother when they escaped to Siberia at the war's beginning. When Harry returned to his hometown after the war, he learned that his father had died of wounds suffered while serving in the Russian army and fighting the Germans. As far as he knew, all of the Schweitzer family had been killed by the Germans as well. Eventually, Harry and his mother and sister made their way to Brooklyn. There, they contacted Jewish organizations in the United States and Israel and placed advertisements in both countries searching for surviving relatives. There were no responses; they were alone. When Sam called me in early 1995, about fifty years after World War II had ended, we wondered together if perhaps there was a connection. He started reading me the given names of his father's Schweitzer father and his father's Schweitzer aunts and uncles. As I heard Sam say Sarah, Leib, Baila, Avraham, Shalom, and Pesach, (the siblings I knew of who had reached adulthood, and whose photos I had in my possession) I felt like I was winning a lottery with no cash value, but with incalculable meaning. The string of names was beyond coincidence and other family details beyond chance. For Sam's father Harry and aunt Luba, it was even more meaningful. Fifty years after thinking they were the only surviving Schweitzers (of their line) in the world, they were suddenly connected to a small family in the US and a much larger family in Israel. By 1996 the Family Finder would be placed online and such "reunions" of families that had been separated by the Shoah would become far from unusual. The local New Jersey newspapers and television news covered the excitement and linkage that a genealogical quest could create.[2] I had the satisfaction of seeing how a research quest could change people's lives.

Most of us grow up with some stories of family origins and this book intentionally does not repeat the tales that I (and my wife's family) grew up with. They are usually routine, occasionally interesting, and sometimes memorable. But those are the stories that came to us without effort. One value of doing work to achieve a goal is that the very act of effort (assuming it does not come with too much pain or suffering) usually makes the achievement all the more meaningful. Therefore, I am sharing a tale of discovery of the stories that our parents didn't tell us: the lost history that our parents' generation didn't even know themselves. In a world where, too often, our independent activities and smart phone, electronic tablet, digital video recorder, and internet lifestyles leave us disconnected from each other, the uncovering of genealogical mysteries and histories we never knew offers the chance of connecting with the broader world in an intimate fashion.

I invite you to join me on that journey.

Chapter 1

☙ A TALE OF A TOMBSTONE ☙

*N*o one knew it then, but with hindsight, we now know that being born Jewish in Poland in the 1920s was a terrible time to have been born Jewish in Poland. After perhaps four hundred years of relative comfort for the Jews of Poland punctuated by rare pogroms and rare accusations of ritual murder, the world of Polish Jewry was about to be snuffed out under the guidance and cruel fist of Nazi Germany.

I do not know what specific factor or factors convinced my grandfather Avraham—my mother's father—to pick up his bags and move from Poland to Tel Aviv, Israel (then Palestine) in 1936. I doubt that he was prescient enough to anticipate the Shoah that would soon wipe out of most of his and my grandmother's families of origin. Had he or others had such clairvoyance, surely the bulk of them would have used every means to leave Poland before the war, rather than stay for what would come. Reading Antony Polonsky's history of *The Jews in Poland and Russia* helped educate me about the growing anti-Jewish feeling that spread in Poland in the pre-war years, particularly noticeable after the death of the Polish leader Józef Piłsudski in 1935. From government quarters, university halls, prominent political parties and from the influential Roman Catholic Church of Poland, hatred of the Jew was increasingly encouraged. The news of a small riot (some called it a pogrom) that led to the death of two Jews in the small Polish town of Przytyk in March 1936 reverberated throughout Polish Jewry and encouraged significant emigration as well.

My grandfather was a deeply religious Zionist. The hope of reestablishing Jewish life in a home where Jews could defend themselves in the once and future land of Israel, combined with the increasing anti-Jewish expressions of feeling and actions in Poland, may well have driven his move. His younger brother Yaakov had emigrated from Poland to Palestine before him, and perhaps his younger brother also provided encouragement. His parents and three of his siblings would be murdered during the Shoah; one sister would survive Auschwitz.

So in 1936 Avraham Tzvi Majzels (pronounced "Mī-zels") moved to Palestine to work for the Jewish National Fund, which planted trees and bought land for Jews in Israel. Separated from his wife and children for two years, by 1938 my grandfather was able to get papers from the British mandate government to allow my mother and uncle and my grandmother to immigrate (make *aliyah*) to Palestine. I found in my mother's papers the Polish passport that my grandmother, mother, and uncle used to travel from Poland to Palestine—on land from Lublin to Romania to Italy, and by boat from Trieste to Palestine. The most critical page contains the September 9, 1938 Warsaw British Passport Office

Visa page from the Polish passport
of Sura Majzels and her children

visa permitting passage to Palestine. Eleven days later they left Poland. On September 25th, they arrived in Palestine at the old Tel Aviv port to begin their new lives. That evening, *Rosh Hashanah*, the Jewish New Year began. The following September Germany invaded Poland.

As I mentioned earlier, during my college years, I became more curious about my family history. And over the years, I asked my mom questions and eventually put together a limited family tree. I had been born an American. My mother had been born in Lublin, Poland. She didn't know exactly where in Poland the birthplace of my grandmother, born Sarah Rozenberg, had been, but my mother thought that my grandmother Sarah had some roots in the Polish village of Markuszów, about 30 kilometers (19 miles) northwest of Lublin.

Rozenberg family tree

My mother did know that my grandmother's father, Icek Erych (Yitzhak Yeroham in Hebrew) Rozenberg was indeed originally from that town of Markuszów. He had died of cancer in 1932 at age forty-seven. Difficult as that must have been, especially at such a relatively early age, I look upon that with relief today knowing that he was spared the horror that he would have otherwise surely lived through and died from. My mother thought that my grandmother's mother, Gitla Rozenberg (née Gewerc) died in Lublin during the Shoah. And there the family history stopped.

After my mother left Poland in 1938, she did not return and thought she never would. After World War II, the few traumatizing post-war pogroms and the not uncommon hostility to the rare surviving

Jews returning to their villages, later followed by a wave of Communist-sponsored anti-Jewish threats and policies in the late 1960s, drove out the vast majority of surviving Jews. It seemed like Poland could never be a place where Jews would visit or live safely and openly again. But, as history often surprises, that would not be the case. The rise of the "Solidarity" trade union and the founding of the first postwar non-Communist government in Poland led to the birth of a New Poland, where Jews again could live a meaningful life, work, and visit in safety.[1]

When my colleague Dr. Walter Reich—a psychiatrist and later head of the United States Holocaust Memorial Museum in Washington, D.C.—convinced me that visits back to Poland were possible in the post-Russian era, I, in turn, convinced my mother to take me on a roots-finding trip back to Poland in the summer of 1993. It was to be her first (and only) trip back there in fifty-five years. Who knew what we might find?

The arrival in Poland was disorienting. This was just a couple years before the internet conquered much of the world, and travel from the West to Poland was not yet routine. East European travel was still an exotic adventure requiring working through obscure travel agencies and pre-paid vouchers for hotel stays that left no flexibility in scheduling. On Walter's advice, we had made arrangements to hire a private guide whom Walter had previously used. The guide was to greet us at Warsaw-Okecie Airport upon our arrival on the overnight LOT Polish Airlines flight from Kennedy Airport in New York. I had some trepidation about identifying ourselves as Jews on a Polish airline, nonetheless I had reserved kosher meals for the flight. Our stewardess was mortified to discover that the plane had not been loaded with our kosher meals and she did her best to find us fresh fruit that could serve as ersatz meals for the flight.

What was disturbing, however, was that when we walked out of Warsaw's airport in a post-overnight daze, there was no guide to greet us. All the detailed advance plans we had made by mail, fax, and phone seemed for nought. Before too long, however, a pleasant fellow named Marco—a Polish Catholic—introduced himself and the driver that he had hired. He indicated that our planned guide had taken ill and had recruited Marco in his absence. We were wary enough at being on what, for my mother and millions of Jews, was the blood-stained soil of Poland, and suddenly the man who had been advertised to us as a guide and protector in Poland and whom we were planning to put our trust in had disappeared and had been replaced by someone who was a stranger to us. Without a viable alternative in this now alien land, our instincts told us to trust this man, and we had a meaningful week of touring Poland with him. I think there remained some wariness on both my mother's and Marco's part, nonetheless. For my mother, Marco symbolized the dark side of Poland's history, when during the pre-war years Jews began to feel increasing anti-Jewish feeling, and when during the actual war years many Poles turned in thousands of Jews who were trying to hide from the Germans who occupied Poland. Of course, there were thousands of Jews who were saved because of the heroism of Righteous Gentiles who risked their lives to hide Jews from the Germans. But in the wake of the millions of Jews who were killed, my mother could not bring herself to think of that perspective. The postwar anti-Jewish feeling in Poland for its first forty-five postwar years only echoed her fears. But Marco soon offered other reasons for her to be wary that full rapprochement between Jews of Polish origin and Christian Poles might not come with ease. One concern was that despite the "new" Poland we were in, even in 1993, Marco was unwilling to take us on a road that passed through the town of Kielce, where a post-Shoah massacre of Jews by Polish Catholics had taken place in 1946. Marco thought that still, forty-seven years after that incident, Kielce was too dangerous a town for Jews even to drive through.

Following a day of regaining our land legs and touring Warsaw, we began our family history excursion. The driver took us on the road from Warsaw to Lublin, which then passed right through Markuszów. Today the new superhighway being built a few kilometers east bypasses the sleepy town entirely.

We knew the Jewish community from Markuszów was long gone, murdered by the Germans in World War II. A village once mostly Jewish, likely was *judenfrei* (Jew-free). According to the historical records,[2] Markuszów (pronounced Mar-*koo*-shoof) had about 1,800 residents in 1921, of whom about 1,000 were Jews. Jews had lived there since at least 1661. The Jewish community grew in the second half of the eighteenth century when Jewish innkeepers, merchants, and craftsmen settled there. A synagogue was established in 1799. In the late nineteenth century, Jewish population growth in Markuszów led the Jewish proportion to double to two-thirds of the population. My great-grandfather Icek Erych Rozenberg, mentioned above, born in 1884, had been in the leather goods business. According to the *Pinkas Hakehillot* encyclopedia of Jewish communities, in the 1930s the economic situation of the Jews of Markuszów had worsened due to an economic boycott on Jewish trade and work by Jew-haters in Poland. Guards were placed before the local shops and stalls of the Jews in 1937, and town Jews felt a threatening atmosphere. In April 1937, nineteen months before Germany would invade Poland, vandals desecrated the Jewish cemetery and smashed fifty gravestones.

The Germans occupied Markuszów on September 11, 1939 and soon established a *Judenrat* (Jewish council) to facilitate their quotas for forced labor and eventual deportations. *"Aktion"*'s of killing Jews began in April 1942 and May 1942 saw a trainload of 1,500 Jews deported to the German-run death camp in Sobibór, Poland. In Markuszów, the Judenrat head Shlomo Goldwasser understood what was planned for the Jews and encouraged his flock to escape to the forests: some became partisans; some just hid there. Within a few months, however, most of the Jews who had fled were found by the Germans (or turned in by local farmers) and killed. Further, with Germans executing Polish farmers who hid or aided Jews, the local Polish Catholic population was, understandably, limited in its willingness and capacity to aid them. Markuszów was relatively unique in the large proportion of Jews (encouraged by Goldwasser) who tried to escape the Nazi grip by fleeing to the forests.[3] It was not unique, however, in that the fate that eventually overtook almost all those escapees was still their murder. After the war, one surviving Jew, Wadya Gluzman, did return to Markuszów and worked there as a carpenter. He is buried in the Markuszów Catholic cemetery today.

In 1993, however, we knew none of the above historical details about Markuszów except that its Jewish community had been destroyed in the Shoah. We wondered as we approached the town if perhaps there would be traces of our roots left in the cemetery. Had it survived? We were quite aware that many Jewish cemeteries had been destroyed by the Germans, with gravestones turned in to paving stones. Even twenty-five years later, as I write this account, there are still some towns in Poland where gravestones are being rehabilitated from paving stones into memorials, and others where the town is reluctant to part with its paving material. We did know that some cemeteries had survived, with potential clues to the past. Marco found the location of the Jewish cemetery in Markuszów and took us there.

Sadly, it had suffered its own fate. Whatever indignities the 1937 desecration of the cemetery had suffered at the hands of local hoodlums, the post-1937 decay was magnitudes greater. After the war, with the Jews gone, what had been a cemetery had become an impassable forest.

Writing this today evokes in me some pain in that Poland is a country whose Roman Catholics (about 95 percent of the population) and Greek Orthodox (some 3 percent of the population) are immensely respectful of cemeteries. On All-Saints Day from corner to corner of Poland, virtually all Poles visit the graves of their ancestors to leave candles and flowers, commune and pray. Poles take great pride in the immaculate condition in which they keep their cemeteries. Their devotion to

Approach to Markuszów
Jewish cemetery
⹖

this puts many other cultures in the world to shame. In contrast to the past decades of disdain, I am grateful that by 2015 the Roman Catholic church in Poland was encouraging Poles to volunteer and help restore the desecrated remaining Jewish cemeteries in Poland out of a respect for the dead of their former neighbors. It is a task, if ever completed, that will take decades. And even in 2016 that Markuszów cemetery remained a thickset forest.

I can assure the reader that for my mother, the idea of searching for roots in the family tree, did not mean literally tripping over roots and climbing through dense bushes. There was simply no way that my mother, then a sixty-four-year-old "proper" European-cultured lady, but always a bit physically frail, was going to hunt for lost tombstones in Indiana Jones style!

We decided to take a walk around the perimeter of the cemetery around the outside low wall, adjacent to the neighbors' agricultural fields, and content ourselves looking in. The three foot high utilitarian concrete barrier that had been erected as a wall perhaps sixty years before was still largely standing to mark off the sacred ground. From the outside it seemed like it would be slim pickings. There were few tombstones to be seen at all; others were barely legible or broken on the ground.

And then, after walking along one of the four sides, we found, standing bright in the sun, just a few feet in from the perimeter wall at the southeast corner of the cemetery, something remarkable: one stone, standing tall amidst a few other dilapidated tombstones. Bright in the sunlight, moss growing a bit on it, a surviving stone that almost seemed to be calling from the past, "remember me." Here, in full glory, stood a possible link to history.

We looked closely at the Hebrew text. Two words seemingly jumped out at us from the bottom of the stone, the line where the identity of the buried person below was revealed: "Sarah Chana," it read. Now these were not two random names, for my grandmother's name—my mother's mother's name—was also Sarah Chana, as shown in the family tree on page 14. When our first child was born, my wife Jeanette and I named her Sarah, in honor of my grandmother Sarah.

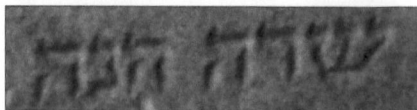

שרה חנה

Sarah Chana's name

My mother and I knew this was *not* my grandmother's tombstone. I knew my grandmother from my childhood; she made it safely to Palestine with my mother in 1938 and I know exactly where she is buried in Israel. I try to visit her tombstone there every year. This stone was not that of my grandmother Sarah Chana. But it was her name. Not just her first name, but both her given names Sarah and Chana.

Tombstone of Sarah Chana

I wondered. I fantasized. Might this be *her* grandmother, the grandmother of my grandmother? As we knew, it was very common in East
Europe for Jews to name children after their deceased ancestors. It would
have made sense for my grandmother Sarah Chana to have been named
after her grandmother Sarah Chana. Was this then my great-great
grandmother's tombstone? But there was no inscribed surname, no last
name, that could have addressed this question in a moment.[4] Sarah and
Chana were common names, and even the combination was not uncommon. It was hard to know. The odds of it being my ancestor's tombstone
would be like finding the proverbial needle in a haystack.

What did we know at that point? My grandmother had emigrated
from Poland to Palestine and lived out her life peacefully in Israel. Her
Markuszów-born father, my great-grandfather, Icek Erych Rozenberg
had died several years before the War and her mother, my great-grandmother, Gitla Rozenberg had been murdered in the Shoah. Could this
tombstone be a missing link to the generation before? I didn't know, but
I wanted to find out.

So the question that I was left with was, "Who was buried in this
Sarah's tomb?" And that is the tale of a tombstone, one that I spent the
next twenty years trying to solve. In hindsight, and with today's internet,
this aspect of my genealogy hobby might have been done in a few days.
But, like all of us, I lacked hindsight before I acquired it, and, in 1993 there
was no publicly-available world-wide web with the resources it has now.

I had a camera with me and took a photo of the stone. Over the
subsequent decades, when I had a free hour or two, I would turn back to
that photo and try to solve the puzzle that it meant to me.

The most prominent feature at the top of the tombstone was what I
immediately assumed to be an open book, perhaps symbolizing knowledge
and specifically study of *Torah*. Growing up in a home where my parents

were both in the first generation in their respective family lines to attend a university, I knew that even without formal academic degrees, learning was respected. My mother always took pride in having had the eminent philosopher Martin Buber as a teacher at the Hebrew University in Jerusalem. Although I wasn't thinking

Open Book

that the Sarah Chana of this tombstone might be a *Yentl*-like character created by Isaac Bashevis Singer and made famous by Barbara Streisand, it didn't seem beyond the pale to me to think that this Sarah Chana might have been a Judaic scholar of sorts. To this day I remain astounded by my mother's response once when I quoted a rhetorical question from the General Prologue of Chaucer's Canterbury Tales, "If gold rusts, what shall iron do?" My mother replied immediately with an antecedent version of the quotation from the Talmud more than a millennium earlier: "If a flame among the cedars fall, what avails the lichen on the wall?"[5] Even if the open book looked like it could be a Pentateuch or Bible (as is presumed to be on the Yale University seal, for example), some wise friends that I later discussed this possibility with in Poland such as Jagellonian University Professor Jonathan Webber and his wife Littman Library Managing Editor Connie Webber or Kraków Rabbi Avi Baumol were skeptical that this Sarah Chana would have been a Yentl, or that a Jewish community of Poland past would have recognized such on a tombstone. Connie had the suggestion that what appeared to be an open book was, in fact, a couple of *"pushke"*s—the ubiquitous coin box Jews use for in-home donations of charity for the poor. This seemed quite possible.

Indeed, one of my childhood memories of visiting my mother's mother Sarah Chana in her tiny apartment in Tel Aviv was of her daily ritual of beginning her morning with placing a coin or two in her *pushke* in the kitchen. Except for the *Shabbat*, the Jewish Sabbath day when she didn't handle money, not a day would go by without her giving a share of what she had to those with less. If my grandmother had been a descendant or relative of the Sarah Chana in question, such behavior would easily have been part of the family tradition. (Of course, such behavior is highly non-specific, and though commendable, was likely part of the daily tradition for many Jewish women of the era.) Yet, when I looked back at other photos I had taken of the tombstone, from different angles, that carving on the headstone was clearly an open book, and not charity boxes!

The other symbol at the head of the tombstone was slightly eroded, but had to be a candlestick. This seemed easy to interpret. It was a quick giveaway to the casual tombstone observer that the grave's occupant was a woman, particularly one whose religious devotion was important to her. Candlesticks that Jewish women traditionally light before *Shabbat* on a tombstone were a common symbol in East Europe. This allusion was not far-fetched. It immediately brought to my mind another image of my past. I vividly remember what turned out to be my last visit to my grandmother Sarah Chana in that same tiny Tel Aviv apartment at the end of December in 1979. By then she was eleven years a widow. Television had come to Israel and part of her Friday afternoon routine was to watch on her small black and white TV set the weekly pre-Sabbath television show broadcast on the only regular TV station at the time. When the Sabbath was about to begin in the late afternoon and the network was accordingly about

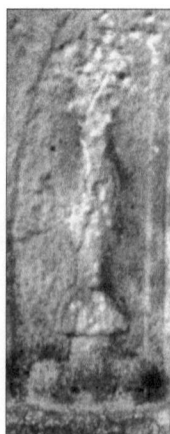

Candlestick

to go off the air, the announcer on the show would end the program by saying to the audience across the airwaves: *"Shabbat Shalom"*—the traditional Hebrew greeting wishing people a peaceful Sabbath. Standing up, my grandmother would look back at the TV announcer and say *"Shabbat Shalom"* back to him, turn off the television, and then light the Sabbath candlesticks on her dining room table, already set for dinner with a white tablecloth. It is always funny to imagine someone talking to a television, especially so in the days before Skype and FaceTime when many of us routinely communicate directly with each other face-to-face across the computer monitor equivalent of television screens. But during sports events people still routinely talk to or scream at their televisions, even though there is no one on the other side to listen or respond. I can imagine that for my widowed grandmother, for whom *Shabbat* was irrevocably different after my grandfather died, the greeting to the TV screen echoed the greeting that she had shared with my grandfather for the forty-five years of their marriage (muted only for the two years that he spent in Palestine in the 1930s working to get permits from the British to bring his wife and children out of Poland).

The Webbers and Rabbi Baumol were taken by the presence of a single candlestick on the tombstone. It was odd for them because, as I mentioned, the traditional *Shabbat* ritual for Jewish women has been to light a *pair* of candlesticks. What was a *single* candlestick doing on a Jewish tombstone? None of them had ever seen anything like that before. After he first saw the photo, Rabbi Baumol kindly introduced me a few weeks later to Warsaw's Monika Krajewska, perhaps the "dean" of East European Jewish tombstone scholars. It was a treat, as I have been in awe of Dr. Krajewska's work since my 1993 Poland trip because of her masterpiece book *A Tribe of Stones*. Intrigued by what this stone meant, my mother bought herself and me copies of the book not long after it was published that same year. A beautifully photographed and explicated collection of Jewish tombstones from throughout East Europe, it opened up the lost world of Jewish cemeteries. Ms. Krajewska kindly responded to my request decades later to look at the tombstone photo and took great interest in the candlestick on the Markuszów tombstone. She had the same reaction. Never in all of her travels and studies had she seen a stone with just one candlestick.

The resolution to that specific mystery that ended up satisfying me turned up, as so many discoveries in our time, through an internet search. Through a Facebook post in 2014, I discovered a wonderful Lublin-based organization called Brama Grodzka Teatr-NN. Established by Tomasz Pietrasiewicz, the "Grodzka Gate" organization has devoted itself for the past twenty-five years to resurrecting the lost history of Lublin as through the centuries. A city that was once more than one-third Jewish is today virtually Jew-free. To maintain the memory of a world that no longer exists Mr. Pietrasiewicz and his colleagues have been heroically trying to hold on to those memories and educate the townspeople of Lublin as to what was lost. On the organization's website, they have posted a collection of glass plate negatives found during a renovation of an attic in a house at Rynek 4 in the *Stare Miasto* (Old City) of Lublin. Likely hidden during the time of the Shoah by photographer Abram Zylberberg, most of the photos are unlabeled. Among them are a haunting collection of tombstones from Jewish cemeteries of Lublin that were largely destroyed during the Second World War.[6] Among these photos are a number of women's tombstones that unquestionably have figures of a single candlestick and a book at the top of the tombstone, such as one from about 1932 of Batsheva Horowitz.[7] In some of these stones, the book is open, facing the viewer, in others closed. In some cases, it is labeled "סידור"

Lublin tombstone of Batsheva Horowitz

(Siddur) to indicate that it represents a Hebrew prayer book. In some cases, it is labeled "ספר" (Sefer) to indicate that it represents a book. In other cases, it is unlabeled. And in one touching case, it is marked with a drawing of a heart! I can conjecture that the use of the prayer book was to represent a devout person and the generic book to represent a learned person. In any case, it is clear that the motif of a single candlestick and a book was not uncommon for Jewish women in the Lublin area before the Second World War, even if it was uncommon or unheard of elsewhere. Perhaps this is the last tombstone of that type that has survived. Perhaps others will be found.

After the "easy" part of looking at the carving on the top of the tombstone came the project that became an intermittent hobby for me for the next twenty years. I felt as if this stone had been waiting for me, and I would make it my slow mission to find out who was buried in Sarah's tomb!

The solution took help from resources all over the world. With the internet, experts are a posting away, and the translation I finally achieved was with the help of the internet and colleagues from the Jewish genealogical website JewishGen.org from around the world. Particularly, I need to acknowledge the help of Yocheved Klausner of Be'er Sheva, Israel, a kind and generous expert in tombstone texts. I could not have done this alone and I continue to learn more, as other experts share with me their insights.

Yocheved Klausner helped me appreciate early in this effort that this tombstone was more than a genealogical record. It was a puzzle left for future generations to solve. She pointed out that the clues to solving the puzzle began right from the first letter of the text.

The wording and placement of the first six lines of the text tell us that a great deal of thought was put into both the word choice for the stone and the precise location of the carving of the letters. Look at the first letter of the first six lines. They spell out the Hebrew letters *Sin-Resh-Heh, Chet-Nun-Heh* (שרה חנה): Sarah Chana's name

Sarah Chana's name in vertical acrostic

in Hebrew. Being a bit playful, the author spells out the deceased's name as introduction to the first six lines of the stone. The author used the ancient Hebrew tradition going back to the Biblical book of Psalms of acrostics—assigning the first letters of lines to spell out hidden meanings, hiding words in the beginning letters of prayers. One of the more famous Hebrew acrostics is the Woman of Valor *"Eshet Chayil"* reading[8] where lines beginning with successive letters of the Hebrew alphabet serve as a mnemonic to help husbands remember the lines of praise traditionally said to honor their wives every Friday night at the Sabbath dinner table.

When I presented a talk about this stone at a Polish *Limmud* educational conference in Fall 2015, Rabbi Baumol pointed out that immediately following the Sarah Chana acrostic is yet another acrostic. The initial letters of the immediately-following three lines of the stone spell out the Hebrew letters *Taf-Nun-Tzadi-Bet-Heh* (תנצבה), a frequently used tombstone abbreviation biblical phrase: "May her soul be bound in the bonds of life."[9] While it might be easy to dismiss such lettering as a coincidence, a close look at the stone shows this bundling of the letters was delib

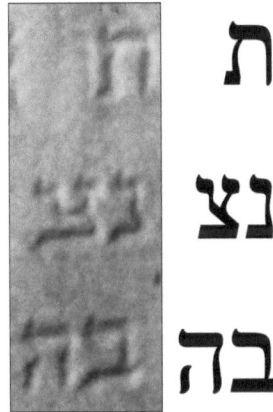

Vertical acrostic from Sarah Chana's tombstone
≈∂

erate. The stonecutter could easily have written the *Bet-Heh* letters in the line before it appears, where there is plenty of space. Instead, the stone cutter dragged out the spacing on that line to permit the acrostic puzzle to continue. This five-letter abbreviation occurs again later. A beautiful rhyming scheme further established the careful planning of content and form that made up the tombstone text.[10]

But who lay in the grave below? My hope was that a line by line analysis would provide the clues to find out. The first line reads:

Listen to us and we shall weep bitterly.	שאו ממנו ונבכה בכי תמרורים

From the first line of text, the composer shares with us the pain this family expressed upon the loss of their relative.[11] The immense grief is palpable.

The second line reads:

Our tears multiply and become like rivers of water.	רבו דמעותינו ויהי לנחלי מים

The overwhelming visual image of their anguish over the family's loss of Sarah Chana echoes the grief the ancient Jewish people experienced after the destruction of the Holy Temple in Jerusalem, as memorialized by the Biblical reference to tears flowing like a river.[12] The third line reads:

Woe! Death has closed our mother's pure eyes.	הה מות סגר עני אמנו הטהורים

And while the mourners' eyes are filled with tears, their mother's pure eyes are permanently closed.

The fourth and fifth lines read:

The sun and moon, constellations, and stars of the sky—	חמה ולבנה מזרות וככבי שמים
their splendor was collected into the darkness and they do not shine upon us.	נגהם נאסף ונחשך ולא יאורי לנו

For the modern genealogist, this is not a routine matter-of-fact epitaph. It is a poetic work of art. Using the Hebrew words for warm "חמה" and white "לבנה" to refer to the sun and moon, respectively, the author not only finds words that allow the creation of the previously mentioned acrostic, but also give biblical texture to the heavenly objects described.[13] In expressing their profound grief, the epitaph's author(s) not only express their immense emotion, but also give that grief a biblical grounding. The sixth and seventh lines read:

Indeed, on the day that the lights were hung,	הלא ביום אשר נתלו המאורות
our glory was taken and lifted from us.	תפארתינו ניטל והורם מאתנו

Again, the imagery is awesome. On one fateful day the bereaved lost the protective, shining light of their Sarah Chana. The eighth line details how they shall express their grief:

Forever we shall remember her,	
for generations and generations!	נצח נזכירה ולדורי דורות

And then, in the ninth line, came the clue that I hoped would solve the mystery of who was buried in Sarah's tomb: the date and year that would permit definite identification—or so I thought:

On the 5th of Marcheshvan, Dalet'	
Lamed Khafsofit, we were left as orphans.	בה מרחשון ד' לך נשארנו יתומים

There is a date there, but it is a cryptic one. In the tenth line we get confirmation that the death took place on that aforementioned date:

For on that day her soul rose to	
the Holy repositories on high.	כי אז עלתה נשמתה לגנזי מרומים

The Hebrew word used here (גנזי, *gin-zey*) for "repositories" is a cognate of the Hebrew word גניזה (*genizah*), which is typically a temporary storage place for books and writings containing the printed name of God. The most famous of these was called to the world's attention in Cairo in the nineteenth century. In using such language on this stone, the bereaved family clearly demonstrated their sense and confidence that her soul could only be destined for permanent linkage to God on high. Finally, for those (such as me, when I first saw the stone) who didn't catch the acrostic of her name at the beginning of the tombstone, we are introduced to the identity of the deceased woman in the eleventh line:

Indeed, it is the woman, modest and straightforward, Mrs.	ה'ה' האשה צנועה וישרה מרת

Following the honorifics,[14] her name is disclosed in the twelfth line:

Sarah Chana, daughter of Reb Chaim Yaakov, Zatzla.	שרה חנה ב'ר חיים יעקב ז'צ'ל'ה

We learn her given name and that of her father and that her father was a man of some renown. The biblically-sourced acronym of *Zatzal* זכר צדיק לברכה, (*zekher tzadik livrakha*) "May the Memory of the Righteous be for a Blessing"[15] is used afer the names of people of outstanding character and behavior. In this case, perhaps for the purpose of completing the rhyming sequence that ends each line, the epitaph writer took the liberty of changing the acronym *Zatzal* to *Zatzla* to have the "hey" letter at the end of this line match the "hey" at the end of the following line.[16] The concluding thirteenth line then provides a critical biographical fact about her father:

Av Bet Din, from here, Markuszów. *May her soul be bound in the bond of the living.*	א'ב'ד' דפה מארקשוו תנצבה

The Hebrew acronym of "א'ב'ד'" (*av bet din*) tells us that her father Chaim Yaakov was the chief rabbi of the local community of Markuszów. Whether in its original Hebrew, or in English translation, this is beautiful poetry. On a fundamental level, it doesn't matter whoever this Sarah was who was buried in Sarah's tomb. She was a remarkable woman.

Once I had gleaned every fact I could from the text and consulted with my sister Daphna, whose Hebrew literacy is exquisite, for any further clues, I started asking other knowledgeable friends. One suggested that I might be able to find out who was Sarah Chana's father: this chief rabbi of Markuszów. He reminded me that there was likely a book about the Jewish history of Markuszów among the memorial volumes written after the Shoah, to recall the lost memories of Jewish life in Europe before the Nazi destruction. So I looked in the Poland volume of *Pinkas Hakehillot*: the record of those Jewish communities. There, on page 316, it clearly stated that in 1880 a Rabbi Chaim Yaakov had served as the rabbi of Markuszów. No start- or end-date to his career, but a specific point in time, at least. Clearly, my mother and I had found *his* daughter's tombstone. Unfortunately, there was no surname, anywhere. Surely, he had one, as surnames were mandatory for use in Poland for most of the nineteenth century.

But now I had a date to work with. Sarah Chana's father was the village rabbi in 1880. Could this Sarah Chana have been connected to me? The dates might fit. I thought my grandmother (also Sarah Chana) had been born in 1903. Could this be the tombstone of *her* grandmother? One could wonder, based on wild estimates of thirty years per generation, that as my grandmother had been born in 1903, her father might have been born around thirty years before then, perhaps around 1873. And my grandmother's grandmother, would have been born about thirty years before that, in 1843. And, by the same set of pure guesswork, if this Rabbi Chaim Yaakov mentioned on the tombstone was her father, then he would have been born in 1813. In 1880 he would have been around age sixty-seven—a reasonable age to be a chief rabbi of a village. So that is all quite possible. But I had to admit: this was all guessing, hand-waving, a theory based on the thinnest of gossamer threads made of flimsy evidence. The names were right. The dates approximately right. But it could all have been coincidence. I needed evidence.

In what was still pre-Facebook times, I posted my dilemma on the JewishGen.org listserv. Colleagues on the listserv correctly focused on the dates. They said: find the dates of interest and then you can solve the mystery. One great idea was to look at the carving on the top of the stone. It was not unusual for Jewish tombstones with arches to have the date of death inscribed along the top. Unfortunately, the carving on the arch had eroded, likely due to the elements or more likely the foliage that dominated the cemetery. With careful "Photoshop" enhancement of a digital image of the stone, I thought I could make out some Hebrew text, identical to what was already on the main epitaph: Died on the fifth of the Hebrew month of *Cheshvan*. But if there ever had been a year carved there, it had worn away in the decades since the stone was placed.

So I still had no year of death and no birth nor married surnames for this Sarah Chana, daughter of Rabbi Chaim Yaakov, Chief Rabbi of Markuszów. This was clearly Rabbi Chaim Yaakov's daughter, but I didn't know his last name. I didn't know her last name. I didn't know if she was my ancestor, or any other living person's, for that matter.

Then came the problem that I wrestled with for years. There *was* one clue to the date carved in the epitaph. What did those Hebrew letters of *Dalet Lamed Chafsofit* in Line 9 mean? I *knew* and those I consulted with were convinced those letters must represent the year. After all, the letters immediately followed the reference to the fifth day of the Hebrew month of *Cheshvan*. So the following phrase must mean the year. It was time for *g'matriya*: the mystical method by which every Hebrew word has a numerical value associated with it. One of the most famous examples is the Hebrew word for life *"chai,"* חי, which is associated with the number 18. That is why, for example, Jews sometimes like numbers that are a multiple of "*chai*," as when one gives a gift based on the number 18, it also carries a subtle wish for good and long life with it.

I consulted with rabbis in the US and Israel. They helped me to solve the *g'matriya* numerology. The Jewish year represented by the letters of *Dalet Lamed Chafsofit* was 5534.[17] That corresponded with the conventional Gregorian calendar year of 1773. But that was an impossible result. First it would mean the tombstone was almost 220 years when I saw it back in 1993. It would have been remarkably well preserved for such an old stone. It is nearly impossible to find stones in the US that are 220 years old that look that good. And this tombstone was in a decayed and nearly destroyed cemetery amidst what had once been war-ravaged Poland. Not only that, it didn't fit with the dates for the daughter of a man who was chief rabbi of Markuszów in 1880. How could his daughter have died in 1773? A further blow to this explanation for the year came from further research I did about the

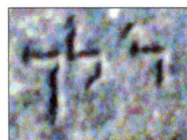

"*Dalet Lamed Chafsofit*" from Sarah Chana's tombstone

cemetery. According to the same records that referred to Rabbi Chaim Yaakov, this cemetery didn't even begin operations until 1855. It made no sense: if the letter-number code of *g'matriya* was correct, this woman died about 1773 while the cemetery didn't open till 1855. Clearly, the logical path I was following was wrong. *Dalet Lamed Chafsofit* was not the Jewish year of 5534. But what was it?

I knew that if I could decipher the riddle of the *Dalet Lamed Chafsofit* letters, I would solve the mystery of who is buried in Sarah's tomb!

Years went by, and I again posted the query on the internet. This time a genealogical colleague offered a brilliant suggestion for how Jews keep track of the year and what that *Dalet Lamed Chafsofit* might represent. The insight was linked to the full date on the tombstone:

On the 5th of Marcheshvan, Dalet' Lamed Khafsofit, we were left as orphans.	בה מרחשון ד׳ לך נשארנו יתומים

There was no question that the first half of the date referred to the fifth day of the month of Hebrew month *Cheshvan* (or *Marcheshvan*, as it is sometimes called), which typically roughly overlaps with November. My colleague suggested that since *Dalet*, using *g'matriya*, is the equivalent of the number 4, perhaps the tombstone was referring to the fourth day of the week: Wednesday. And further, the Hebrew letters *Lamed Khafsofit* (לך) were an abbreviation for the weekly *Torah* portion of *Lech L'cha*, suggesting the death took place on a Wednesday during the week when the *Torah* portion of *Lech L'cha* (Genesis 12:1–17:27) is read in synagogue. This hypothesis was intriguing. Indeed, every week in the year is associated with a specific *Torah* reading. Traditional Jews sometimes did refer to a week by its corresponding Torah portion. If I could prove that this Sarah Chana indeed died on a Wednesday when *Lech L'cha* was being read, I could likely find a record of her death in the Polish State Archives without having to search through hundreds of hand-written texts in a Russian or Polish language I could barely read.[18] I still didn't know the year, but this was a clue, if I could prove that this woman in this tomb died on a Wednesday of *Lech L'cha* and that my ancestor had died in that small town on that day, it had to be her.

But who was my great-great-grandmother? I still didn't know. Because of the fracture in time caused by the Shoah, the family history passed on to my mother had stopped prior to the generation of the woman of the epitaph. Following an internet search for a possible partner in this quest, I contacted a Catholic historian of Polish Jewry at one of the universities in Lublin to see if he might be willing to permit me to hire him to search the Polish State Archives for the Jewish records of Markuszów for further clues. He was too busy with his own work, but kindly referred me to an independent Lublin scholar named Paweł Sygowski. I consider Mr. Sygowski, whom I now am privileged to call Paweł, a great hero. His English language skills then were not quite as limited as my Polish language competence. But with the help of Google translate, I was able to correspond with him by email in a relatively coherent fashion. Today those Polish archives have all been digitized, and with some effort, are available at no charge for those with some competence in the original languages. I have since learned to do rudimentary searches myself. But as recently as a few years ago, digital copies of the original documents were unavailable.

To give Paweł some focus, I asked him to find all the Rozenberg records he could find from the town of Markuszów, expecting that some would surely be related to the Rozenberg family of my great-grandfather and myself. Might any have been possibly connected with the Sarah Chana tombstone?

The first ray of hope came when Paweł emailed me a typed copy of my great-grandfather's 1884 birth record from Markuszów. Paweł translated the original Russian into Polish, and with Google's help, I translated the Polish into English that I could understand:

"On 20 December 1884 Icek Erych, the son of Lejba Rozenberg— tradesman (age 38) and Sura Hana (age 36) née Kohen was born." Icek is the Polish spelling for Yitzhak (Isaac), my great-grandfather's given name. Lejba is the Polish spelling for Leib—who was clearly my great-great grandfather. And Sura Hana is the Polish spelling for Sarah Chana, who had to be my great-great grandmother. And my great-great grandmother now had a surname as well: Kohen.

When I look at the online copy of that birth record in the Polish State Archives today, even though my capacity to read old hand-written

Birth record of Icek Erych Rozenberg

Russian is virtually nil, I can clearly make out the bold cursive writing of my great-grandfather's name Izach Erych in the eleventh line of the document.

At that point, I clearly had smashed through what genealogists call a "brick wall"—a previously unbreachable limit in the search for family history. I now knew who my great-great-grandparents were. But what about the tombstone? I still could not prove that *my* Sarah Chana and the Sarah Chana buried under the tombstone were both the same woman.

Fortunately, with the same work effort, Mr. Sygowski was also able to find the Markuszów death record for *my* Sarah Chana. I've underlined the family names on this record. My Google-assisted translation of his abbreviated Polish translation of the original Russian

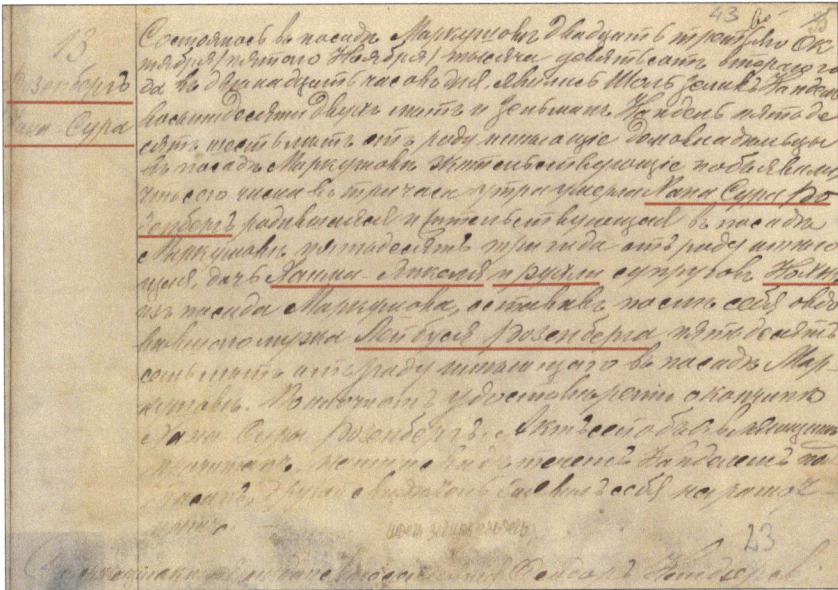

Death record of Sarah Chana Rozenberg

reads: "On November 5, 1902 Shol Zelig Kandel (age 82) and Zelman Kandel (age 53) came to the recording office in Markuszów as witnesses and they reported that the female Markuszów resident Chana Sarah Rozenberg (age 56) died today. She was the daughter of Chaim Jankiel Kohen and his wife Ruchla of Markuszów and is survived by her husband Lejbus Rozenberg (age 57)."

This record provided powerful information. It refers to a Chana Sarah, who surely could be Sarah Chana Rozenberg, whom I had just learned *was* my great-great grandmother. This Chana Sarah died on November 5, 1902. This Chana Sarah is clearly my great-great grandmother, as she is recorded as having left behind her husband Leib Rozenberg as her widower. But are all these Sarah Chana records concerning the very same woman as in the grave we had found? The civil record says that her father was Chaim Yankiel Kohen. The tombstone says that

Sarah Chana's father was Chaim Yaakov. As Yankiel is a Yiddish nickname for Yaakov, Chaim Yankiel is clearly Chaim Yaakov. It seemed that this tombstone was indeed that of my great-grandmother, and now I had learned not only her name, but the name of her husband and her parents. I had cracked the code!

To prove this unequivocally, however, the dates all needed to match. What did I know at this point? The archival death record said my ancestor Sura Chana, daughter of Chaim Yankiel, died on November 5, 1902. The tombstone said that this woman died on the 5th of the Hebrew month of *Cheshvan*. So the key question left was whether November 5, 1902 was also the 5th of *Cheshvan*. The internet had the answer. In this case, the website hebcal.com was the source. Entering 5 November 1902 into their Hebrew date converter (you can try this yourself), the corresponding Hebrew date of 5th of *Cheshvan* 5663 immediately popped up. But there were more details that needed confirmation to be absolutely sure. Recall that one interpretation of the epitaph implied that she died on a Wednesday, the fourth day of the week. Was the 5th of November, 1902 a Wednesday? That same hebcal.com site gave a positive match: November 5, 1902 was indeed a Wednesday. So that left one last detail to confirm if everything truly matched: Was November 5, 1902 a day during the one week of that entire year named so because Jews around the world read from the *Lech L'cha* portion of the *Torah*? If so, it would be a perfect match. Again, according to hebcal.com, November 5, 1902 was the Wednesday during the week when *Lech L'cha* was read by Jews around the world.[19]

I will skip the statistics calculations here, but the chances were now proven better than 99.999999% that these were not coincidences and that my mother and I had stumbled upon the miraculously surviving burial stone and place of my great-great grandmother Sarah Chana Rozenberg.

I don't think any of us are this sure of about much of anything else in life, so I was satisfied I had the answer.

Within the two years after Sarah Chana Rozenberg's death, her son—my great-grandfather Icek—married my great-grandmother Gitla and gave birth to my grandmother. Fittingly, she was named Sarah Chana Rozenberg as well.

I began this story with my mother. But, in my mind, genealogy means little, however, unless one can pass it on. And that was my remaining challenge. The tombstone reads "Forever we shall remember her, for generations and generations." How could I make that possible?

My opportunity came in the summer of 2013. I had planned to make a trip back to Poland for my scientific research and I invited my younger daughter Amalyah to join me for a side trip to share with her our past. There we faced the greatest research challenge. Our hosts, a wonderful Catholic Polish couple (Dean and Professor Marek Koziorowski and Dr. Anna Koziorowska of the University of Rzeszów) happily took us to the Markuszów cemetery so that I could show the stone to Amalyah. My question then was, would we be able to find it? At that point, I hadn't been there in twenty years and was fuzzy in my memory of how to get there. I knew from the Polish Jewish History museum "Virtual Shtetl" website where the cemetery was located and my hosts took us there, off of Łachy Street, in Markuszów. But the situation was quite serious. The cemetery was even more overgrown. It had become a densely forested jungle. By the time of day we arrived, it was growing dark and prospects were dismal. We found a few hidden stones scattered in the woods, but finding *the* tombstone seemed hopeless; we found nothing. My friend and colleague Marek wouldn't let us despair. After all, he said, he was a hunter, and able to track things down. We spent an hour in the bramble-filled woods and found nothing.

I was carrying silent, hidden tears that afternoon on the drive home. I had brought Amalyah halfway around the world—in large part for this—and had failed. Twenty years earlier, without knowing it, I had found my great-great grandmother's tombstone, but it was now lost.

What had gone wrong? Had the stone been destroyed over the twenty years since I had been there with my mother in 1993? Had the inevitable plant growth hidden it? Nothing lives forever, except for what we choose to retain in our collective memory, so how could I rely on a physical stone?

But I had come too far and was not ready to give up. And while I might return to Poland for my scientific research, the odds were that my daughter, whose life was in America, would never come back to Poland again. I did not want to fail.

I returned to my hosts' home that evening knowing that I had one last day in Poland with Amalyah before our departure. I went back to the internet and looked at that map of the graveyard and noted how we had entered. Google was again a critical resource. I went to the Google Maps website to find that location to get a birds' eye view of the cemetery.

There I saw how we had entered from Łachy street. I wondered, if, lost in the woods to the east of Łachy, perhaps we had failed to explore the area completely. I remembered from 1993 that the stone was near the perimeter. Then, I saw there was another way in. From the main street: Lubelska. That was how my mother and I had found the stone twenty years before. I looked at the street view from Google. This was the entrance I had remembered in my mind (see photo on page 19). Twenty years later, the forest of trees was still visible at the end of a now-paved driveway.

We simply had to go back. I quickly went online and arranged to rent a car the next day, with a GPS so we wouldn't get lost. I drove

ABOVE: Google Earth Pro View of Markuszów Jewish cemetery area.

BELOW: Virtual Shtetl/Google Map of Markuszów Jewish cemetery area.

ɘʊ

RIGHT: Google Street View of entrance
to Markusów Jewish cemetery.

ɘʊ

Amalyah back to the cemetery and in the fading light of that day reached there. We proceeded to hunt for that stone from the other direction. Within a few minutes from a new angle I saw out of the left side of my eye the stone I had spent twenty years trying to decipher and had brought my daughter halfway around the world to find. It was obscured by the trees, but still standing tall. The stone of my grandmother's grandmother Sarah Chana Rozenberg—daughter of Rabbi Chaim Yaakov Hacohen and Ruchel of Markuszów—a remarkable woman worthy of remembrance.

And then, in a tradition of tombstone followers throughout the world, Amalyah made a rubbing (tracing with pencil onto paper) of some of the words at the top of the stone and could make a hands-on connection to her great-great-great-grandmother, five generations before her, born 141 years before her. And that Sarah Chana would never be forgotten in her life. I have since learned that doing stone rubbings is not necessarily wise, because in the process of doing a rubbing one can hasten the stone's natural deterioration! I won't do it again, and I won't do it on any other stone I find. Yet even this one will need to be replaced someday.

I will conclude this story, however, by returning to the poetry of the stone. The *Torah* portion of *Lech L'cha* mentioned on Sarah's tomb comes from the Book of Genesis and solved one mystery. There remain more. Reviewing the text, I can ask, "Were all those flowery words at the top of the tombstone just beautiful poetry?," or was the writer who composed that epitaph trying to teach us something? I think the answer is found elsewhere in the Book of Genesis (1: 14–19):

And God said, "Let there be luminaries in the expanse of the heavens,
to separate between the day and between the night, and they shall be
for signs and for appointed seasons and for days and years.

Amalyah Oren rubbing tombstone

And they shall be for luminaries in the expanse of the heavens to shed light upon the earth." And it was so.

And God made the two great luminaries: the great luminary to rule the day and the lesser luminary to rule the night, and the stars.

And God placed them in the expanse of the heavens to shed light upon the earth.

And to rule over the day and over the night, and to separate between the light and between the darkness, and God saw that it was good.

And it was evening, and it was morning, a fourth day.

Now look back at the text that I was struggling with on Sarah Chana's epitaph:

The sun and moon, constellations, and stars of the sky

Their splendor was collected into darkness and they do not shine
upon us

Indeed, on the same day that the lights were hung,

Our glory was taken and lifted from us.

What was this poetry telling us? I believe that the tombstone is referring us to the section from Genesis where we just read about the day of creation, when the sun and moon, constellations and stars were hung in the sky: the *fourth* day. The fourth day of the week, the *Dalet* day of the week: Wednesday. The tombstone was crying out to us that on a Wednesday, the very same day that God had created the sun and the moon, the constellations and stars, on a Wednesday, the Wednesday of the week that the *Torah* portion that *Lech L'cha* was read, Sarah Chana was taken away. The poetry told of us a Wednesday and a woman that her family hoped would never be forgotten.[20]

Chapter 2

❧ Two Horses in Lublin ❧

*F*ollowing my mother's and my arrival in Poland in 1993, we were most excited about visiting her hometown of Lublin. She had left at age nine. What still remained? In a city that brought death to her relatives, would there be anything to remind her of home? We knew that most of what had once been the Jewish quarter of Lublin had been torn down in postwar urban renewal under the Soviet-dominated Polish government.

But that was not to be the case in the neighborhood where my mother had lived, just outside the Jewish quarter: on Grodzka street, the central street of the *Stare Miasto*, the "old city" of Lublin. Grodzka Street (meaning "Town Street") is thought to be the oldest street in Lublin, dating back at least to the city's founding in 1317. In the early twentieth century, perhaps one-third of the occupants of that *Stare Miasto* neighbor-

ABOVE: Grodzka Street, Lublin, looking northeast (1920s)

BELOW: Grodzka Street (1993)

∾

hood were Jews. The 1920s photo at left shows how it had looked in my mother's memories of the years before World War II. Amazingly, it was all still there. Though Jews had been killed by the tens of thousands in Lublin and its surroundings, and there was damage to the city when the German conquered the town in 1939, Lublin had not been a prominent battleground during World War II. In my 1993 photo the street looked surprisingly similar to its earlier appearance. The 11 Grodzka building (on the far right of the pre-war photo and again in cream color in the middle of the 1993 photo on the right side of the street) had served as the Lublin Jewish orphanage and home for the elderly until the war. In a story parallel to that famous one of Dr. Janusz Korczak's heroism in Warsaw's Jewish orphanage, the Germans removed and killed the Lublin orphanage occupants and the staff who chose to stay with their wards. Across the open park (that my mother recalled playing in as a child) from the orphanage building, we found 7 Grodzka, where my mother had spent her first nine years of life. To the right of the orphanage, in the 1993 photo the salmon and red-pink color double-entranced building (shown bounded by an old woman on the cobblestones and a young boy on a ledge) contained my mother's apartment. In a large multi-family building, her family lived in one apartment and numerous cousins, aunts, and uncles lived in the others.

We entered the courtyard. In a daze induced by her first steps inside her home building in fifty-five years, the awareness that the building had survived the terrible war, the painful knowledge that most of those who had lived there were murdered, and a touch of jet lag, my mother let the moment absorb her. She pointed out the balcony where her father would build a traditional *"sukkah"* booth every fall for the *Sukkot* holiday. The inner courtyard apartments were now mostly empty except for a government office. My mother said the ghosts of those who had lived there were still inhab-

Rebeka Oren in the courtyard
of 7 Grodzka (1993)

iting the place. Though much of the building is used today, each time I would return over subsequent decades, I still had the sense that the ghosts are still living there. On one of my subsequent visits I found an open back door to the building and breathlessly entered the hallway my mother and grandparents had walked each day in their youth. On the floor lay gorgeous primitive mosaics, presumably dating back to the better times in Lublin before World War II. A colorful peacock was particularly striking.[1]

On that original day of visiting the building, our guide Marco was kind enough to help my mother and me find the city Monument Conservation Department and trace the provenance of the building a bit. According to those records, because most of my mother's family had been killed during the Shoah, the property was transferred to the Polish national treasury. Marco, however, was quick to put us, from his perspective, in our place. Some of the building was now being used by a government social service office. It would be a terrible thing, he said, if we were to claim the building back from those needy people who made use of its public services today. While my mother never filed a claim for the home she had been a child in over the following final twenty-three years

Floor mosaic in Rebeka Oren's entry to 7 Grodzka

of her life nor had she ever expressed to me the slightest interest in such a possibility, prior to that moment on her family's onetime grounds, I had not known the meaning that filing such claims for "restitution" had for Poles. In fact, the displacements and expulsions of World War II and its aftermath challenges the provenance of building ownership throughout Poland to this day.

Perhaps hundreds of thousands of Jewish-owned properties were never fairly or properly adjudicated postwar. With Polish people having moved into formerly Jewish-owned properties, either voluntarily or by German or Soviet-led resettlement, the process of confronting the issues of "who suffered more," or, as the Talmud would put it, "whose blood is redder" is full of pain and few fully satisfying resolutions. Threatening actions by Polish residents and neighbors towards returning surviving Jews and the need to fight to reclaim rights to Jewish-owned property surely made many Jewish survivors of the Shoah eager to wash their hands and their memories of whatever good life had existed for them in Poland before the war.[2] Of perhaps several thousand Lublin Jews who had survived the war (mostly by escaping to Siberia) and then returned to Lublin, the majority had left Poland in the six years after the war, mostly due to the anti-Jewish attitudes or violence carried out by their neighbors upon their return, and even more so after the Polish pogrom against Jews in Kielce in 1946.[3] That does not mean that the majority of Christian neighbors were threatening towards returning Jews, but, as in any neighborhood, it only takes a small proportion of threatening or violent people to poison an atmosphere and make a neighborhood unwelcome or unsafe. There were surely far too few neighbors protecting or welcoming the Jewish returnees for most of those returnees to feel safe. In the thriving economy that Poland has experienced over its twenty-five years following the years of Soviet influence, the capitalism-induced rising values of land and property has only made the issue even more charged for Jews and non-Jews alike. On our 1993 visit, despite our guide's ambivalence about our presence, we walked through the courtyard, talked our way for a moment into the social service office that occupied the space where my mother had once lived, looked around, and then went on our way.

The doorway in front of 7 Grodzka was a touchstone for my future visits to Poland. When I returned with my daughter Amalyah exactly twenty years later, it was a spot of pilgrimage to show her part of her heri-

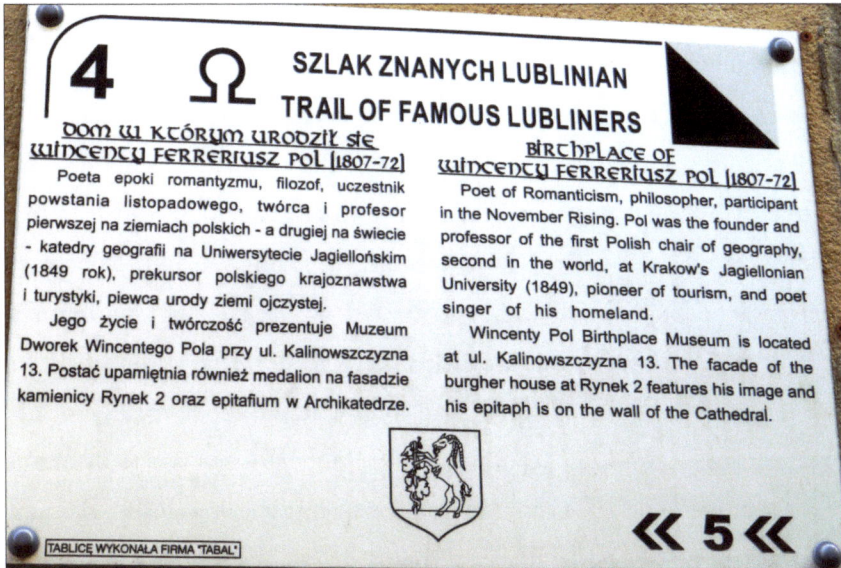

Plaque at main entrance to 7 Grodzka (2013)

tage. On subsequent trips, I would proudly take my wife and older daughter Sarah and on another occasion my sister and her two older children to see this link to the past. A plaque on the outside of the building noted the location's place in Polish history, as the spot where romantic poet Wincenty Pol had been born in 1807. Curiously, and this will assume more curiosity later, there was no visible evidence that a Jewish man had built the building, that his family had lived there for a few decades, and that they were murdered under the German occupation during the years of the Shoah. It was as if a central piece of this building's history had been erased from the public record.

My interest in the building was rekindled in the fall of 2014, during my year living in Poland as a Fulbright Researcher at the University of Rzeszów in southeast Poland. One weekend I stayed in the historic and glorious town of Kraków, following a lecture I gave at the Kraków Jewish Community Center in the historically Jewish "Kazimierz" section of the city. The building and its community are an amazing story in their own right. Led by the tireless and creative American-Israeli-Pole named Jonathan Ornstein (partnering with the wise and genial Rabbi Avi Baumol), built with the support and endorsement of Britain's Prince Charles, and staffed by an energetic crew of Polish Jews and fifty non-Jewish Polish volunteers nicknamed "the Meshugoyim" (a lovingly playful construct merging the Yiddish words for crazy and non-Jews), the building is a seed of hope and rebirth amidst the otherwise desolate history for Jews in most of Poland. I had gone there to give a talk about the tale of my great-great grandmother's tombstone. As Rabbi Baumol was to be out of town that weekend, as a courtesy to me as guest speaker, Rabbi Baumol and Jonathan Ornstein permitted me to stay in the rabbi's JCC-owned Kazimierz apartment for the weekend.

Finding myself with some time to relax on Saturday afternoon, I took the liberty of perusing the bookshelves of Rabbi Baumol's apartment looking for something to stimulate my mind. My eyes were drawn to a copy of the "Atlas of Polish Jewish History," published by the Jewish Historical Institute of Poland, located in Warsaw. Though the book was entirely written in Polish, of which my knowledge was limited, it was first of all an atlas: a book of maps and charts. Filled with pictures, it was sufficient for me to explore with modest comprehension.

I turned through the pages and looked at the maps of various towns and cities in Poland, particularly keeping my eye out for mention of Lublin. When I got to the page showing the Lublin ghetto during the Shoah years, my jaw dropped.

In the lower part of the ghetto (demarcated by a red border), the numeral "1" was located in the exact spot (at the corner of Grodzka and Archidiakońska streets) where my mother's apartment was located.[4] I looked at the index to the page and saw that "1" was designated as the

2
3
Unicka Street

Czwartek

Lubartowska Street

Wysoka
Św. Mikołaja
Krzywa
Ruska
Targowa
Ruska

Pl.
Targowy
4

Cmentarz
Żydowski

Futmiańska
Nadstawna
Szeroka
Jateczna
Ostowa

Cyrulicza

Zamkowa
Zamek
Podzamcze
Wąska

Kowalska
Brama
Grodzka
Krawiecka

Rybna
Archidiakońska
1

Bramowa
Grodzka

Złota
RYNEK
Dominikańska
Jezuicka

Królewska
Podwale

———	Ghetto border March 1941
	Ghetto A February 1942
▬	Ghetto B February 1942
1	Judenrat
2	Yeshivat Chachmei Lublin
———	Route of Jewish Deportation

Lublin ghetto map

location of the *Judenrat*—the infamous Jewish councils that the Nazis implemented in Jewish communities throughout Poland to serve as local insiders to facilitate the Nazi demands upon those captured Jews. Initially providing social service work to the local communities, as the war progressed, those *Judenrats* generally came to play the role of organizing forced labor call-ups, eventually aiding in the assembly of local Jews for forced deportations to other towns or to the Nazi death camps.

Returning to the shock of the moment in 2014, however, I was stunned then to learn that my mother's home had some seventy years earlier housed the Lublin *Judenrat*. Again, one would find no plaque on the building indicating such an awful fate had befallen my mother's home. My mother surely had never heard that such a thing had happened. Else she would definitely have told me about it at some point during our forty-seven years on Earth together. This surprising new information led me to return to an old question of what had become of the rest of the family that lived there.

On that line of my family, I knew that my mother had been born in Lublin to Sarah Chana Majzels (née Rozenberg). Sarah Chana's father had been Icek Erych Rozenberg (son of the Sarah Chana of the tombstone story). And Sarah Chana's mother had been Gitla (Gitaleh) Rozenberg (née Gewerc). My mother, who knew Gitaleh before the war, had told me that Gitaleh was a religious woman whose sense of personal modesty led her to avoid having her photos taken. The photo of her

Icek Erych ROZENBERG & Gitla GEWERC

Sara (Sura) Chana ROZENBERG

Rebeka MAYZELS

Dan OREN

Rozenberg family tree

in the family tree is the only one of which I know. Icek Erych had died of natural causes several years before the war, and my mother recalled that Gitaleh still lived in one apartment in that 7 Grodzka building, and that several other Rozenberg/Gewerc-related families lived in other apartments in the same building. But what exactly happened to those relatives, and what had happened specifically to my great-grandmother Gitaleh during the war was largely unknown besides their not having survived. This made for another compelling mystery.

My mother recalled that Gitaleh and Icek had six children who had reached adulthood. (There were others who likely did not survive past infancy.) The oldest one—the only one who escaped Poland and the Nazis before the war—was my grandmother Sarah Chana. Her younger sister Cypa was born about 1906 and was thought killed in the Shoah about 1942. The next sister was Henia, born in 1909 and a survivor of Maidanek and Auschwitz death camps, who moved to Israel after the

ABOVE:
Cypa and husband Eliezer Goberman

RIGHT:
Henia Rozenberg

war. Married before the war, she lost her first husband and their son to the Shoah. Her son Moshe (from a second marriage after the war) did not learn of his mother's prior family until years after she died, when he saw a testimony that she had submitted to the Yad Vashem Shoah memorial institute in Jerusalem. I remember Henia vividly from a family visit to Israel in 1968. In those years when tattoos were uncommon (except on military men!), the numbers on her arm from her Auschwitz experi-

Siblings Batsheva and
Chaim Rozenberg

ence were a vivid permanent scar that still sears my memory. Brother Chaim was born in 1912, ordained as a rabbi, trained and practiced as a lawyer, survived the war and died in 1972. My mother thought that he had lost the love of his life in the war, and he never married afterwards. The next sibling was sister Batsheva (shown left of Chaim in the photo above of them strolling), born in 1916. She was likely murdered about 1941 or 1942. There was another, Ester, about whom I know nothing more than a birth year of 1918. And there was a younger brother Wulf, born in 1921, who was killed in the Shoah in 1942.

As for the matron of the family, my great-grandmother Gitaleh had been born in the Wieniawa (Chekhov) section of Lublin in 1883 and also died about 1942. Knowing that it was her home that became the site of the *Judenrat*, I was now especially interested to learn her fate along with that of her house.

If one walks down to the end of the block in the earlier photos to Grodzka Gate (*"Brama Grodzka"* in Polish)—today a Lublin historical research and teaching institute run by Tomasz Pietrasiewicz—one can learn more about 7 Grodzka. Pietrasiewicz (called Tomek by friends and colleagues) is surely a beacon of light in our era, if ever there was one. About the same time that my mother and I visited Lublin, Tomek decided to found a theatrical company ("TEATR NN") there. Much to his surprise—in a city that had been largely "scrubbed" of Jews, first by the murderous actions of the Germans, and then by the hostility of post-war Poles and then by governmental erasure of history—Tomek and his colleagues found a history of a 700-year-old town with a long and strong Jewish presence, with Jews making up one-third of the Lublin population as late as the early twentieth century. The space the city had given Tomek and colleagues to create their theater company—the "Grodzka Gate" building lay a 140 yard walk down a gentle hill from my mother's apartment—was perched on the edge of the demolished Jewish quarter and its lost past. With that suppressed knowledge staring Tomek and his colleagues in the face, they created a City of Lublin-sponsored institution that, to this day, makes sure even if there are only a handful of Jews left in Lublin, that truth not be denied its place.

A centerpiece of their physical displays is a reconstructed three-dimensional diorama of the Old City of Lublin. I took a photo of it and marked the two streets that limit the apartment building on the complex of Grodzka and Archidiakońska streets. Next to what was once a park and today bares the ruins of a medieval church, it occupies a prominent spot in the old city.

Among the Grodzka Gate collections are the records they are assembling of every building in the *Stare Miasto* of Lublin before the war. Eventually they hope to expand that to include the story of every

Location of 7 Grodzka complex in the Old City diorama,
Grodzka Gate, Lublin
ह

Jew who lived in Lublin before the war. In a heroic effort, their staff are combing through the Polish State Archives in Lublin to document in proper fashion the physical history of the old city. In documenting the physical history, the human history emerges. A search of their records began to open for me the sad, but in a slight way heart-warming, story of my great-grandmother's fate.

The building is listed at the *Brama Grodzka* as number 6 Archidiakońska street (as it is on the corner of Archidiakońska and Grodzka). According to those records it was built at the beginning of the twentieth century by Wulf Gewerc (Gitaleh's father), and after World War II it became the property of the Polish State Treasury because "the entire family" had been killed.

I later hired researcher Tadeusz Przystojecki to help me unravel the ownership record of the building, initially owned by my great-great grandparents Wulf and Szejwa Bracha Gewerc. I would learn that Wulf must have been a very successful contractor in the increasingly decrepit town of Wieniawa (then adjacent to and now part of) Lublin. At the start of the twentieth century, he had bought the prime land at the heart of the Old City of Lublin and gave apartments at 7 Grodzka to his children. As far as I know, ten of their children in an era of still widespread child mortality survived to adulthood, including my great-grandmother Gitaleh (Gitel), shown at right, as with her sisters with their married surnames.

Nine of the ten were still living when World War II broke out, and together with the family of their by-then-deceased brother Abram, were the heirs and legal

Gewerc family tree

owners of 7 Grodzka at the time. All would be murdered in the Shoah. So when the court records at one point referred to "the entire Gewerc family" having been killed, they were correct to a large degree: virtually the entire generation of Wulf and Szejwa Bracha Gewerc's children indeed perished.

I was particularly eager to learn what had happened to my great-grandmother Gitaleh. To my shock and tearful joy, the researchers at *Brama Grodzka* had some of that story in their files. From *Brama Grodzka*, I learned that the *Judenrat* records of April 19, 1940 mention the family building and my great-grandmother by name (presented here in English translation):

The Management Board of the Jewish Community . . . states that it received 1 pair of horses about eight years old . . . from Gitla Gewerc, residing at 7 Grodzka street. The horses will be used by the Jewish community as a pulling force [for delivering food and supplies to refugees, displaced persons, and poor local Jews]. . . . Mrs. Gitla Gewerc will not receive any remuneration for the use of these horses. In case of death of, or damage to the . . . horses, the municipality is obligated to pay Mrs. Gitla Gewerc either a relevant compensation or the return of other horses of the same quality. These horses should be returned to Mrs. Gitla Gewerc with at least two months' notice. In case of a request by Mrs. Gitla Gewerc resulting in failure by the Jewish community to return the horses, the municipality must pay Mrs. Gitla Gewerc 50 złoty per day.

It brought me some meaningful comfort to know that my great-grand-mother—clearly a woman of some means, daughter of the contractor who built the apartment block, and owner of at least two horses—was pitching in to support the Jewish community of Lublin at an hour of tremendous need.

She would have been fifty-seven at the time, seeing the world fall apart around her. By the next month, if not already earlier, she was surely witnessing even more severe pressures. The *Judenrat* records of May 5, 1940 two weeks later state that it had established its Office of Forced Labor (for women) at 7 Grodzka street. I can imagine the horror she was experiencing as she saw her family's apartment building turned into an instrument of Nazi oppression. On July 4, 1940, the *Judenrat* issued a statement calling on all Jewish women aged sixteen to sixty years to report within six days for mandatory job assignment to the 7 Grodzka Office of Forced Labor for Women and to pay a registration fee for this privilege. Those who did not register voluntarily were warned they would be taken by force to a local labor camp.

While I was pleased to learn, through those and other records, that none of my family names were listed as having been members of the Lublin *Judenrat*, and I would like to imagine that my ancestors and their siblings would have refused to serve as agents of German oppression, I realize that the *Judenrat* was trying to make the best of a forced living nightmare throughout Nazi Eastern Europe. A proper evaluation of those councils is beyond the scope of this recounting but suffice it to say that the roles that the council members were placed in—torn between trying to save their communities and trying to serve the German masters—surely created moral challenges that I would wish on no one. Some *Judenrat* members were surely saints in their time, and some may well have danced with the devil. To this day, I remain grateful that I have never been forced into such a dilemma.

On October 2, 1940, following the arrival of Jewish prisoners in Lublin *from* the Belzec labor camp and their confinement in a different labor camp in Lublin, the 7 Grodzka office was used as a collection spot for food and clothing parcel donations for those deportees. Apparently, the Germans had ordered that relatives of those Jews not be permitted to have direct contact with the prisoners and that the *Judenrat* serve as a conduit for supplying the prisoners' food and clothing needs. The *Judenrat* emphasized that attempts by family members to venture near the labor camp (on Lindenstrasse in Lublin) and have direct contact with those prisoners would possibly lead the family members to be imprisoned as well. The German terror apparatus effectively spread its tentacles wide across society.

Through the *Brama Grodzka* records, I learned that by March 16 of the following year, the *Judenrat's* Registration of Persons Office was

also located within the 7 Grodzka Street building. This office was established for registration of all the Jews who then were being coerced by
the Germans through the *Judenrat* to volunteer for deportations out of
Lublin. The incentive for going voluntarily on these deportations was
supposedly to gain better treatment and more privileges than would
be given to those who waited for later involuntary deportations. Those
on the deportations would then also avoid being part of the formally-
established Lublin ghetto.

On April 3 and 10, 1941 the *Judenrat* recorded 7 Grodzka as the
site for distribution of vouchers that could be exchanged for matzahs for
the upcoming Passover holiday beginning on April 11.

And what became of my great-grandmother Gitaleh? This new
understanding of the fate of her home and two of the livestock she owned
led me to investigate her history again. JewishGen.org continually is
updating its online database, and a new search one day produced a record
I had never encountered previously. Looking for people whose surnames
were phonetically like Rozenberg and whose given names were phonetically like Gitaleh, I found a match for Gitla Rozenberg on a list of Jews
who had been "voluntarily" deported from Lublin. This Gitla had been
born in 1883 and was deported on March 18, 1941 to the destination of
Siedliszcze. At last, seventy-three years after Gitaleh had disappeared off
the face of the earth, I had some inkling of her fate. Judging by the March
16, 1941 date of the *Judenrat* announcement promoting the voluntary
deportations right from her own front door, and the March 18 date of the
official record of her deportation to the tiny village of Siedliszcze, (which
on that date had no ghetto) some twenty-six miles east of Lublin, I have
a guess at her final outcome. In the Polish State Archives in Lublin is a
copy of the original document indexed on the JewishGen website. On
that copy of the Siedliszcze deportation list, her name (and birth year)

appear as deportee number 1210, immediately above the name of her daughter Szewa (Batsheva). From this dual listing, I derive some tiny bit of comfort knowing that in this certain hour of tragedy, at least she was not alone.

Records from the US Holocaust Memorial Museum indicate that the "voluntary" resettlement was one of about a dozen conducted by the German authorities in March 1941 in order to create more space for the German army and to create unoccupied space for a Jewish ghetto in Lublin. A formal announcement of the creation of the Jewish ghetto in Lublin was made on March 24, 1941.[5]

Detailed explorations of the Siedliszcze voluntary deportation database showed me that elsewhere on this roster, in addition to Gitaleh's daughter, her brothers Chaim Szloma, Dawid, and Lejb, her sister Sura, and her niece Szprincza were listed. From these datapoints, I can reconstruct the possible scenario that with their home apartments at 7 Grodzka being steadily taken from them, there was nothing left for the extended family in Lublin. Perhaps fantasizing along with the other 1,800 Lublin ghetto residents who would be deported to Siedliszcze on March eighteenth that a better situation might await them, many of the Gewerc family members, including my great-grandmother, left Lublin as a group.

The YIVO Institute for Jewish Research in New York City has a photo depicting a group of people on a cart on one of the deportations from Lublin.

It is easy to imagine that the adult woman with the hooded coat marked with a Shield of David ("Jewish star") looking straight at the camera is my great-grandmother Gitaleh as part of the March 18, 1941 deportation group. The people on the cart are dressed for a winter's day in Poland. They appear to have luggage as would be consistent with the

Jews being deported from Lublin

voluntary deportations. They do not seem to be expressing quite the level of duress and fear that might be associated with deportations to labor camps or unknown potentially fatal destinations. And, perhaps providing a fitting destiny to her prior action, even the two horses pulling the cart in the photo are the two horses that Gitaleh had lent to the Lublin Jewish community one year earlier? Of course, such speculations about the photograph are likely fantasies. That woman could just as well have been anybody's great-grandmother and the cart could have been taking the deportees to any of more than dozens of destinations. Conjecture or not, the photo allowed my imagination to run.

Gitaleh's personal fate beyond that date remains entirely unknown. While writing this chapter, I met with David Silberklang, Ph.D., researcher at the Yad Vashem Holocaust Museum in Jerusalem and author of a book about the German murder of Jews in the Lublin region.

Mr. Silberklang explained to me that as part of this set of "voluntary" deportations from Lublin, thousands of Jews were essentially "dumped" onto a number of tiny Jewish communities nearby that surely could not have had the resources to provide adequate food and shelter to the massive numbers of new immigrants. Siedliszcze had approximately 700 Jews prior to the Shoah. The sudden wartime arrival of another 1,800 residents to the Jewish community would surely have been overwhelming. By the time of the liquidation of the Siedliszcze ghetto in October, 1942, virtually all of the Jews deported from Lublin who might still have been alive there would likely have been killed or deported to their destiny at the Sobibór death camp.[6]

I would later learn from Mr. Przystojecki, the researcher whom I had hired, that Gitaleh's son Chaim (and my great uncle), who had survived the war in hiding in Siberia, went back to Lublin after the war. Back in Poland, Chaim filed legal claims and successfully recovered his late mother's share of the property before leaving Poland for good. He sold his shares to non-Jewish Poles in 1949.[7] In impoverished postwar Poland under Soviet influence, the financial value of the property at that time was likely minimal. Though I now know that my mother never had a financial claim to the building herself (so there was no need for our guide to worry that my mother might file a claim on it), my hope of a historical claim remains undiminished. One day, perhaps, a plaque on the building will recognize the history of the building both for the Jewish souls who once lived there, and for the perversion of history that Germany imposed upon its residents and upon its use. As for the two horses Gitaleh had lent to support the needy of the Lublin ghetto, I presume the animals were never returned.

Chapter 3

❧ PATRIMONY ❧

*A*long my genealogical journey, I decided to explore the family roots of my wife, born Jeanette Kuvin. As with any voyage of learning, it is a never-ending quest. For a spouse to tolerate the other spouse's hobbies (or obsessions as they sometimes become) takes patience and generosity. I thought that if I also explored Jeanette's family history alongside my own, I might evoke interest in my hobby. And, when we had children, I continued in this task, so that one day I could give our kids both of their parents' histories as a gift in the form of "their genealogy" and not just "my genealogy." It has been more than thirty years now since I began exploring Jeanette's family history, and I'll leave it to her to address whether I succeeded in evoking her tolerance for my obsessive interest in our family's genealogy. The definitive answer to that question won't be in this book, but I'd like to think that at least on a few occasions I've succeeded.

As with most genealogical inquiries, I started with a surname: Kuvin, Jeanette's last name. As opposed to more "typical" names of Jews, such as Greenbaum or Cohen or Levine, Kuvin not only did not sound particularly Jewish nor European but was exceptionally rare. I had never known of another Kuvin nor had even heard of the surname Kuvin until I met Jeanette.

Jeanette and her father Sandy (Sanford) knew well the recent lineage of their surname Kuvin. Sandy's mother had been born Freda Kuvin in Newark, New Jersey, in 1899.[1] After the death of Sandy's father Jacob Fleishfarb eleven years into his marriage to Freda, Freda returned to using Kuvin as her family name. Surely, Kuvin was less noticeably Jewish-sounding than Fleishfarb, and it connected her more closely to her parents who were both still living. Beyond that simple story, however, when I asked about it in the mid-1980s, Sandy knew little about the origins of the Kuvin name or his exact family history. He had known Kuvin, Fleishfarb, Seife, Peck and Roth as among the jumble of surnames of his relatives, but the connections were obscure. There was one exception, however. Going back to Sandy's childhood days in Newark of the 1930s, Sandy had been friends with his second cousin, Philip, about three years younger than him. Sandy and Philip shared the same set of great-grandparents, unknown to Sandy except for the same surname. Decades after they had played as children and decades after both had left Newark for their respective accomplishments in life, they would still talk together by phone on rare occasions and laugh as they chanted their favorite cheer from Newark's predominantly Jewish Weequahic High School:

"Ikey, Mikey, Jakey, Sam,
We're the boys that eat no ham,
We play baseball, we play soccer,
We keep matzos in our lockers
Aye, Yiye, Yiye, Yiye, Weequahic High!"

But I get ahead of myself. I'll return to Sandy Kuvin and his second cousin named Philip *Roth* soon.

I still own my 1985 copy of the Yale University Alumni Directory. In the pre-internet era in which it was published, the alumni directory was indispensable to my research of Yale history at the time. Its 1,424 pages contained the name, address and telephone number where available, and Yale degree of virtually every living graduate of the university. For all practical purposes, it was a direct pathway to the world.

I purchased the volume as soon as the Association of Yale Alumni had published it and for cheap entertainment one evening I suggested to Jeanette that we look up if there were any living Kuvins who had been graduated from Yale. (My assumption then and now was that Jeanette, Master of Public Health graduate Class of 1985 was the first in Yale's history.) On page 453 I found there was one living Yale alumnus with the Kuvin surname—a certain Leonard Kuvin. According to the directory, Leonard Kuvin had been enrolled in the graduate school at Yale in the mid-1920s, though it did not seem that he had received a degree from Yale. Some sixty years later, he was listed as retired and living in Florida. Leonard's name was unknown to Jeanette. I asked her father Sandy if the name meant anything to him. He replied from a cloudy memory that Leonard was possibly a distant relative, but he just wasn't sure if he had ever met him or if he really knew who Leonard was at all.

The alumni directory provided me with Leonard's telephone number, so I picked up the phone and dialed him. When I reached the then eighty-five-year-old, Leonard was not pleased to take my unexpected call and uninterested in the subject matter. I explained that I was married to Jeanette, the daughter of Sandy Kuvin, originally from Newark, and that I was working on our family history. I told him that I wasn't sure if he was related but I was hoping to speak with him to explore possibilities. He was civil but made it clear that he was unwilling to speak further. Before I would disconnect, however, I indicated that I would send him a letter to try and pursue the subject further.

Such a reaction by Leonard to my cold call is not unusual in the course of genealogy hunting. Even before the current era when most of us with telephones dread the barrage of telemarketers and robocalls that invade our privacy, exploit our good will, and waste our time, people interested in pursuing genealogy by phone would often be rebuffed. Some people called would refuse, thinking that the so-called "long-lost relative" was searching for money. Others would refuse because family history was something they were trying to avoid and not consider. Familiar with the territory, and amidst my training then as a psychiatrist to find ways to explore people's personal history, I was disappointed but not rebuffed.

As I had indicated to Leonard in the phone call, I composed a letter to him, repeating my connection to Jeanette and her father Sandy Kuvin, and sought to engage Leonard in finding if he had a connection to my Kuvin relatives. I would never hear back from Leonard. At least not directly.

Five years would pass by until one day I received an unexpected letter in the mail from Leonard's daughter, Joan Kuvin Olsson. A quick phone call to her led her to share with me a fascinating, and not so uncommon story in histories of Jewish, or once-Jewish, families.

As Joan explained to me, she had been a content, middle-aged wife and mother living in the US on December 30, 1990 when she sat down to read *The New York Times*. In that day's *Magazine*, an adapted section was excerpted from the final chapter of Philip Roth's upcoming book *Patrimony*, the story of Philip's father Herman Roth's final illness and what it evoked in Philip and Herman. Of every section the editors could have chosen to promote the new book in the *Magazine*, they happened to select a section that began the article with a paragraph in which the only full name mentioned was that of Philip's second cousin Sandy Kuvin:

> Just about a year after my father was diagnosed as having a brain tumor, he began, all at once, to lose his equilibrium. In the meantime, he'd had a cataract removed—restoring to his left eye practically 20/20 vision—and he and his companion, Lil, had gone to Florida for their usual stay of four months. In December, in Palm Beach, they even attended the wedding that our cousin, Sandy Kuvin, had invited him to the previous spring, back when the brain surgeon had told me that unless we okayed a hazardous operation, in a relatively short time he'd be much worse off—back when I thought that he'd never see Florida again.[2]

For Joan, daughter of by-then ninety-year-old Leonard Kuvin, of self-proclaimed French Protestant Huguenot descent, reading this Philip Roth paragraph could not have been more jarring. For the Philip Roth who wrote this excerpt was nothing less than *the* Philip Roth, considered by many to be one of the greatest authors of our time. Philip's writings often drew from the American Jewish experience, and this excerpt was no less clear in highlighting the immigrant Jewish origins of Philip's parents and, by association, of cousin Sandy Kuvin.

Joan's parents had raised her to think that "Kuvin" was an old French Protestant name (perhaps pronounced historically as the French might, "Koo-van"). Her father had told her that he had no relatives from his family of origin, consequently there was no one around to dispel the myth as she grew up to adulthood. This article by Philip Roth, the first time she was encountering the Kuvin name outside her family of origin, made her suspicious that the story of origin that had guided her childhood was suspect. Impulsively, she sent off a letter to Philip to investigate further. Right afterwards she telephoned her father in Florida to confront him about a history that she now assumed was fabricated. As she later wrote, her father's initial response was to dismiss her suspicions as those of a "fantasy-ridden lunatic."

She persisted and demanded her very elderly father share his secrets. Within twenty-four hours, the floodgates opened. In the coming days and weeks, by phone, and then in person, he would share his many recollections of a rich Jewish/Yiddish heritage. That heritage had long ago been hidden—from his colleagues and his own family— and he cultivated a cover set of lies (as Joan wrote later) in order to succeed educationally and professionally in the genteel anti-Jewish world he had encountered in the America of the 1920s. Though the risk of pogroms and anti-Jewish violence had not poisoned the US as it had stained Europe over the centuries, for much of the twentieth century American Jews faced social, economic, and occupational prejudices. (Such barriers were, of course, not unique to Jews and were surely experienced to greater or lesser degrees by other "minority" groups as well.) Some Jews found, however, that they could potentially escape the limitations they faced in social and professional opportunities by avoiding, or in Leonard's case, hiding their Jewish background. Such stories involving ancestors of former US Secretaries of State Madeline

Albright and John Kerry or current Princeton University president Christopher Eisgruber pop up in the news media every few years and echo this phenomenon. As a graduate student in economics at Yale in the 1920s, the era when Yale College instituted its informal "Limitations on Numbers of Jewish Students" quota and when its university faculty rarely would consider hiring a Jew and less so promoting him to high rank, Leonard was surely sensitive to the prevailing zeitgeist. In his mind, as for many others at Yale and across the US, success in America would mean putting his Judaism behind him and sealing off that history from the children he would sire.

Soon after confronting her father by telephone, Joan visited him in person to uncover her lost history. Together Joan and Leonard read *Patrimony*, a book all about an elderly Jewish father and his middle-aged child. Leonard entertained Joan "royally" (as she recalled it) with anecdotes and Yiddish expressions he had not used for nearly eighty years. She later wrote me how satisfying it was for her to understand her paternal background and how she thought it had brought her father "a world of good to finally reveal his past and to make peace with it." Indeed, as the two talked in person, he pulled out from a hidden corner the letter I had sent him some five years earlier to inquire about a Jewish Kuvin connection. That letter provided Joan the link to reach out to me. Though I can't speak for Leonard's psyche at the time, the fact that he had held on to my letter for those five years, and still knew where to find it, suggested that despite the decades of obfuscation, he could not fully forget his origins. As with any letter or object we keep for posterity, it may either serve to remind us of a past event, or offer guidance about our state of mind to our heirs.

With my letter and background information in her and her father's hands, Joan and her father helped me build a more complete Roth family tree, of which a partial view appears below. Joan, Philip, and Sandy were all second cousins and descendants of Akiva and Sara Roth of Kozłów, a small town in the Ternopil district of today's Ukraine, formerly within the province of Galicia during the Austro-Hungarian empire and later within the borders of Poland.

This chapter began with musings about the unusual surname of Kuvin. By the time I began inquiring about its origins, no one whom I knew in the family had any real knowledge of its origins in "the old country." Sandy Kuvin thought that the family had come from Tarnopol, a variant name for today's Ternopil. But we didn't know. In the mid-1990s, when I first got home access to the "World Wide Web" and was able to gain access to the amazing Jewish Records Indexing-Poland (JRI-Poland) searchable online database, I looked for Kuvins from Tarnopol.

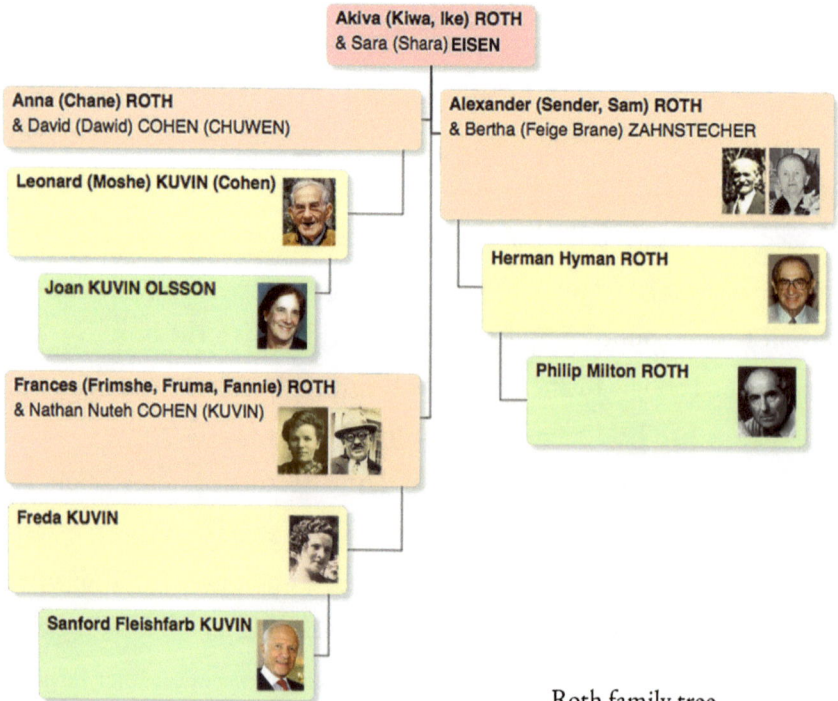

Roth family tree

Then and now, the search was fruitless. The name remained a proverbial "brick wall" of non-information.

Ninety-year old Leonard Kuvin provided the answer. Joan reported that as part of her father's disclosure of his hidden past, his memory was that Kuvin was a variation of the former name of "Chauvin." That insight changed everything in my Kuvin hunt. As of this chapter's writing for example, when one searches for phonetically similar surnames to "Chauvin" from the "Tarnopol" district in the JRI-Poland database, 181 archival records come up, mostly of people with the surname "Chuwen." Pay dirt! With the guttural sound of an East European "Ch" equivalent to the Hebrew "chet" and then Americanized to the sound of an American "K," the Polish "w" pronounced in English like an American "v," and the "en" at surname's end Americanized to its equivalent "in," "Chuwen" in Galicia seamlessly became "Kuvin" in America. From this jumping-off point, I could now begin to explore the history of the Chuwens in Europe and the Kuvins in the United States. In the US, the future would prove bright.

Joan also learned from her father about the stresses of his immigrant childhood. Leonard's parents had died young when he was still in his early teens. Orphaned and impoverished, he was left to sleep on park benches or temporarily with a kind sibling. His sisters then encouraged him to Americanize his name from Chuwen to Kuvin before entering graduate school at Yale in order to have an easier professional life.

Some four years after Joan and I first corresponded, Leonard passed away at the age of ninety-four in 1995. Over the two decades since, we have been in contact on a few occasions, sometimes trading a bit of newly found genealogical data. Joan proved eager to communicate with me and recover the ancestral links of which she had been deprived. While she was truly shocked by her potential discovery through *The New York*

Times back then, in today's extraordinary world of information avail-
ability, whether by Google's surveying the web or Wikileaks dumping
of private files, true secrets are few and such discoveries are made every
day. Anyone with a surname of Kuvin could enter that name on a Google search (and I suspect few of us have not looked for our name on an
internet search at some point) and quickly find significant Jewish Kuvin
connections. That does not prove that all Kuvins are Jews; indeed, today
a good number are not. But in America, at least, almost all of the Kuvins
I've found online are of at least partial Jewish heritage. And in our era
when so much genealogical information has already been posted on sites
such as Ancestry.com and Geni.com, entering the name Kuvin would
quickly lead an inquisitive family member to find their heritage, whether
Leonard or a different ancestor had wanted that hidden or not. DNA
testing adds new such discoveries as well. Of course, just because something appears on a database or on the internet does not mean it is true.
Indeed, some sites that rely on personal report and hearsay, rather than
strict documentation, are particularly prone to error, be it through typo-
graphical errors or sloppy record-keeping.

In the years after *Patrimony* was published, Philip donated his correspondence, including his personal family correspondence, to the Library
of Congress in Washington, D.C., where it is all in the public domain
for research purposes. Consequently, the Kuvin story of this chapter is
already available to the world, due in part to Joan's letters and Leonard's
own insights. In time a different relative, whom I'll call George, from
another branch of the Kuvin (but not the Roth) side of Jeanette's family
would contact me regarding his tentative and bewildering-to-him discovery that his Newark-born grandfather had also been of Jewish origin.
As he wrote at the time, "I never had any ties to anything or anyone of
the Jewish faith or background . . . All of my family have been brought

up in a Christian environment (Presbyterian)." To his further surprise, after further exploration, I was able to confirm that George, too, was descended from Chuwens and that he was a distant relative by marriage of the same Roth family above. His Newark-born grandfather had dissociated himself from his Jewish family and married outside the Jewish faith in 1925, a time when such intermarriages were rare, unlike the current era when perhaps half of all Jews in the US marry outside the faith. His Chuwen ancestors hailed from the same general area of Tarnopol, Galicia that Leonard Kuvin's family had come from and his Chuwen great-great grandparents were the same Chuwen great-great grandparents of Jeanette, making George and my wife Jeanette third cousins of each other. For whatever reasons, whether it was assimilating from visible Judaism into the American background noise or avoiding the tension of intermarriage in a family that frowned on it, the hiding of past Jewish identity was not so unusual in the story of American Jews. For Philip Roth, the question of what is Jewish identity and the phenomenon of passing oneself as something else were integral to his oeuvre. For the extended Chuwen/Kuvin families in America, these issues were no less germane. The protagonist of Roth's novel *The Human Stain*, published in 2000, is an African American who spends his professional career passing as a Jew. Though Roth later wrote that the book was inspired by an incident in the life of a friend of his who was a professor at Princeton, I sometimes wonder whether Joan Kuvin Olsson's discovery of her father Leonard Kuvin's record of hiding his background, which she shared with Philip in 1991, might also have informed that work.

A Roth cousin in England (a son of a different second cousin of Philip's) recently shared with me the apocryphal story of a distant relative of Philip's who had tracked him down and went to visit Philip at his home. Philip answered the door when the relative arrived and she told him that she was his cousin. According to the anecdote, Philip's answer was, "So what?" Fortunately for my wife, she had better luck with the famously reclusive author. As previously noted, Philip and Jeanette's father Sandy had remained in occasional and friendly contact through their adulthood, especially in the latter decades of their lives. Beyond chanting "Ikey, Mikey, Jakey, Sam . . . ," at the time when Philip's father Herman was undergoing treatment for his final illness, Philip would sometimes consult with physician Sandy. When Philip was researching medical illness for his 2006 novel *Everyman,* he called on Sandy for medical guidance. When Jeanette contacted Philip in 2008 to propose a meeting, he graciously accepted our invitation for him to be our guest for dinner with us and our two teenage daughters at a New York Upper West Side kosher restaurant. He was kind and friendly. As our girls could speak freely as typical adolescents, while their parents could just sit in awe of being with the renowned writer (even if to Jeanette he was cousin Philip), I think he found their company more entertaining than ours. At the least, Philip—childless as far as I know—seemed quite interested in how and what young people thought.

To my relief, Philip even seemed a bit interested in learning more about his own genealogy, of which he knew very little. In his literary autobiography *The Facts,* he recalled that his childhood inquiries about his family's pre-American days had been met at home with a "willful amnesia."[3] I showed him a chart I had prepared of the Roth family tree. When he saw a box on the chart depicting his then publicly rarely-mentioned first fraught marriage to Margaret Martinson Williams, (who had apparently tricked him into a difficult relationship and marriage throughout the nearly one decade of its existence),[4] he looked at me and, referring to his then-deceased first wife, asked me "What's *she* doing there?" Philip offered no objection to seeing the family tree depict his then-ended five-year marriage to the renowned actress Claire Bloom. Though I never expunged Ms. Williams from my own records, I made sure that when I later mailed Philip an updated copy of the family tree, that version did not include his first marriage. At some point over the next fifteen years, however, Philip must have come to terms with people recognizing Ms. Williams as part of his personal narrative as a person, as a writer and as a Jew, and would confide such to his biographer.[5]

When I look at the Roth family tree that I have assembled, I see that from one couple, Akiva Roth and Sara Eisen who lived and died in the mid-nineteenth century town of Kozłów in Tarnopol Province, Galicia (today's Ukraine), 384 descendants whom I know of would one day be born. Surely there are more out there, waiting to be surprised by their hidden lineage.

Chapter 4

⁕ Laocoön and his Sons ⁕

My wife Jeanette's family had been shaped by and always conscious of the Shoah. Indeed, her mother Gaby and Gaby's parents Henry and Edith Townsend (formerly Heinz and Edith Taubenschlag) narrowly escaped Nazi German clutches before reaching the safe shores of New York in April 1939. Heinz had been a successful physician in Berlin and his wife Edith (née Pollak) brought to the marriage the lineage of being a granddaughter of Hermann Leiser, cofounder of the famous Leiser shoe chain in Europe.

Edith, or "Oma" (German for grandmother) as everyone in the family called her, was always a sweet, gentle and kind woman. In retrospect, Jeanette has wondered if Oma might also have been suffering from clinical depression for most of her life, at least during the years that Jeanette knew her as her grandmother. Oma's taking antidepressant medication during the last few years of her life at least gave her some relief at that time. I am not in a position to write about whatever inner psychological issues she struggled with that might have contributed to her depression, but the sociological stresses she faced were overwhelming. Sadly, during the time of the Shoah, these were not unique.

After Oma died at age ninety in 1997, her daughter Gaby found Oma's diary of her pre-marriage years and had it translated from the original German into English. Out of respect for her mother's privacy, Gaby never read the contents. Out of my interest in history and family genealogy, with Gaby's permission, I later did. There was nothing salacious to be found and the contents were what one would expect to see in the writings of a young woman in her late teens and early twenties as she interacted with her family and dated men until she found her "Mr. Right." One reads the story of a family that was fully conscious and practicing of liberal Judaism, at least in terms of celebrating Sabbath dinners and the High Holidays, yet also fully part of the secular German world, marking Christmas time with a tree in the home. The men she records dating were Jewish, and one even went on to become a prominent Reform rabbi. She also records having a delightful time in the late 1920s visiting her Jewish relatives in Prague, Czechoslovakia, birthplace of her father Maximilian (Max) Pollak.

As with most of the Jews of Germany in the 1930s, the rise of Hitler and the Nazi Party in Germany was beyond Oma's Pollak family's imagination. Jews had been loyal citizens and loyal soldiers of the Kaiser's Army during the First World War, and they thought their position in German society secure. When Edith Pollak married Heinz Taubenschlag on April 21, 1929 at the tail end of the Roaring Twenties, the great US stock market crash six months later that would trigger a worldwide

"Great Depression" profoundly affecting the US and Germany was also beyond their vision.

The gradual destruction of Jewish rights in Germany in the 1930s associated with the rise of Hitler seemed to them like a temporary aberration that would abate. The relative security of a doctor's steady income and whatever money her parents might have given her from the family shoe business surely protected Edith and Heinz from the suffering German economy. Through much of the decade they remained blind to the fate that awaited them and their family. Even a 1933 anti-Jewish boycott against Jewish businesses throughout the Germany, including their Leiser family shoe chain, did not raise sufficient personal concern.

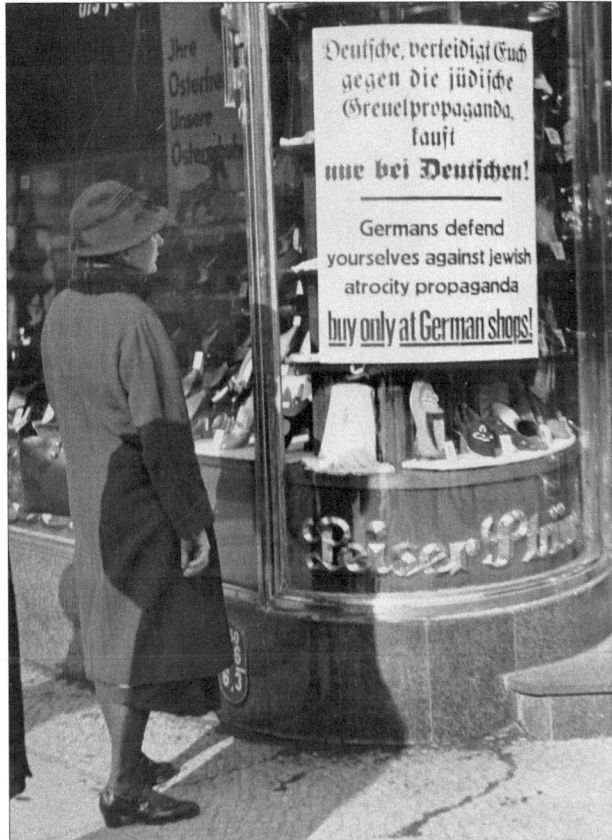

Boycott sign at
Leiser Shoes, Berlin
(April 1, 1933)

Ruins of the Fasanenstrasse Synagogue, Berlin (April 16, 1941)

❧

The turning point for Edith and Heinz came in 1938. German discrimination against Jews specifically targeted those in the professions. By June, Jewish doctors were no longer permitted to treat Aryan patients. By the end of September, they were forbidden from practicing at all as physicians. Heinz felt concerned enough by the restrictions that, fearing arrest, he went into hiding, frequently changing locations. Krystallnacht (the "Night of Broken Glass") shattered that innocence throughout German Jewry. Across Germany and Austria on November 9–10, 1938, German forces and civilians ransacked Jewish homes, hospitals, and schools. Over 1,000 synagogues were burned, including the great Fasanenstrasse Synagogue (above) in Berlin where Edith and Heinz had been married almost a decade before. Hundreds of Jews were murdered during the pogroms, and 30,000 more Jews were arrested and imprisoned in German concentration camps. The brutal assault was followed by the government fining the German Jewish community for all the associated damages to public property.

Edith and Heinz finally realized that they needed to flee Germany. Within weeks Edith had a new passport that would allow her to leave Germany for any country willing to take her. Prominently stamped with a red "J" for "Jude," the December 30, 1938 document with the Nazi eagle and swastika testifies to the chronological connection between Krystallnacht and the impetus to depart. This passport allows us to recon-

German Passport of
Edith Taubenschlag

struct what was surely a harrowing passage of two months' time during which Edith and Heinz must have worried daily about where they could flee safely and whether they could do so before Hitler's next round of anti-Jewish violence—sure to be even worse than Krystallnacht—would be unleashed. Surely, they wrestled with how to protect their three-year-old daughter Gaby and their seven-year-old son Peter from the terror around them. They decided to go against the long odds for success and apply for entry to the United States of America. Perhaps because Heinz was a physician, and thereby offered a useful skill to the US and was

US Quota Immigration Visa of Edith Taubenschlag

therefore unlikely to become an unemployed financial burden on a country burdened with its own deep economic recession, Heinz and Edith were granted quota immigration visas by Cyrus B. Follmer, US Vice Consul in Berlin, on March 2, 1939. Edith later suggested that a bribe to the right American official also aided in her getting the visa for the family. Whatever created the tipping point for these soon-to-be refugees, they now had a potential escape route from the Nazi menace in Europe.

As the passport stamps record, Heinz and Edith rushed to leave Germany and four days later they were at the Berlin-Tempelhof airport for a flight to Amsterdam. The Ellis Island immigration records show that after three weeks in Amsterdam, the family of four was able to board the S.S. Veendam from Rotterdam on March 25, 1938 and arrived in the US eleven days later. A 16-millimeter black and white movie that Heinz filmed and we recently found in a storage room shows their ship steaming into the New York Harbor, with the Statue of Liberty offering hope above them.[1] Heinz's parents Richard and Rosalie could not get paperwork to leave. Richard and Rosalie would be deported from Berlin to the Warsaw Ghetto on April 2, 1942. Richard died within two months there. Rosalie was killed about three months after deportation, having been sent from Warsaw as a prisoner to the Trawniki forced labor camp near Lublin. Edith's father Max Pollak had died of natural causes in 1936. Edith's mother Fella (née Leiser) Pollak clung to the hope that her position in Germany would be safe and refused to leave Germany with Heinz and Edith. Later she fled with a few other Leiser family relatives to the momentary relative enclave of Amsterdam. But she would be arrested in Amsterdam on March 3, 1943 and incarcerated in the Scheveningen police prison. Seven months later she was deported to Auschwitz on October 19, 1943, where she, too, was murdered.

It is easy to imagine the losses that Edith suffered during the Shoah as having contributed to her dysphoria. Her mother and one of her brothers were murdered by Germany, as were her in-laws as well. A comfortable pre-war life had been shattered. Naturally, neither she nor daughter Gaby nor son Peter could talk about the events and losses of the Shoah without intense emotion, and they usually preferred not to talk about them at all. Strangely, to me at least, Edith's ingrained German identity postwar still allowed her to carry a love or at least fond memories of some her favorite locations and stores of Berlin. But she never spoke about the family who had been torn away forever.

I began my serious inquiries into Jeanette's family's genealogy after Oma (Edith) had passed away. And with her gone there was no one left who might have had a clue to her father's Prague-born side of her family. What we knew of the Pollaks stopped with Max Pollak.

An opportunity to investigate further came in 2010 when Jeanette and I decided to take a brief trip to the historic city of Prague. Today the records of the Prague Jewish communities are all available online through the Czech National Archives website, though navigating them is not for the faint of heart. At the time of our visit, they were not online, however, and we were kindly assisted by archival researcher Lenka

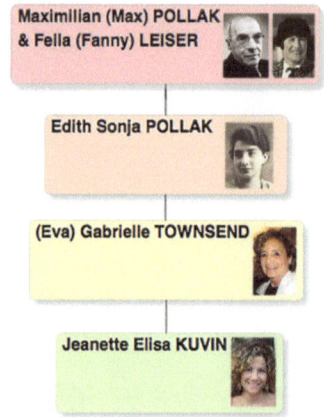

ABOVE: Max Pollak family tree

BELOW: Abraham Pollak family tree

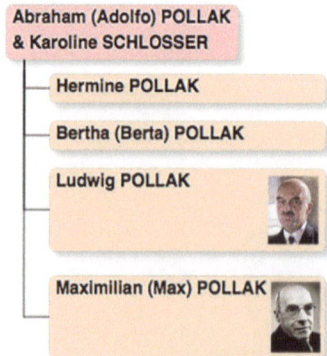

Matusikova, Ph.D. who was supervising the digitization of those records. No one knew those registers as she did and she promised to investigate for us.

What she found opened the door to a precious history. Max, she reported, was the youngest of four children born to Abraham Pollak and Karoline (née Schlosser) Pollak.[2] Those children were Hermine (born 1861), Bertha (born 1866), Ludwig (born 1868), and Max (born 1870). Suddenly some unknown names in Edith's diary from 1924 and 1925 had meaning to me. When Edith referred to visiting the "Wurms," she was visiting the home of her Aunt Hermine, who had married Julius Wurm. Hermine died in 1926. When Edith referred to having a good time with Aunt Bertha, she was writing of another sister of her father's. The Czech Holocaust Archives database records that Bertha was transported from Prague to the Terezin concentration camp (the German showplace camp for propaganda purposes) outside of the city on July 6, 1942. The same database records her again being transported on December 15, 1943 from Terezin to Auschwitz, where she met her final fate. But Ludwig's name does not appear in Edith's diary.

Indeed, soon after, when I asked Edith's children Gaby and Peter (by then septuagenarians themselves) neither recognized the name of Ludwig, nor Bertha, nor Hermine. They had no recollection of their mother ever having even mentioned the existence of any siblings of her father. Clearly, Edith had personally known at least two of the three, and after I learned more about Ludwig, the less likely it seemed that she could not have not at least known who he was by name, even if she might never have met him. In retrospect, the fate of those siblings, or at least that of Bertha and Ludwig may have been too painful for Edith to share.

A genealogist or a genealogy-hunter considers it a bonus when searching Google and finding a website with a few sentences or a paragraph about a new-found relative. When I googled Ludwig Pollak, I hit the proverbial jackpot in that not only were there links to a few sentences, there were links to website after website about him. It seemed too good to be true, and I wasn't willing to believe that our "Ludwig Pollak" was the same as the famous "Ludwig Pollak" on the internet until after I could get corroborating information about names, city and year of birth that proved that Ludwig Pollak and Maximillian Pollak had to have been brothers. A side by side comparison of a painting of art historian Ludwig Pollak next to a photograph of Max shows a striking similarity but was not sufficient proof.

Most critically, Google led me to an entire book written about Ludwig Pollak by historian Margarete Merkel Guldan as part of her doctoral dissertation. Her edited version of his diaries provides the lion's share of what we know about Ludwig today. When I walked into Yale

ABOVE LEFT: Painting of Ludwig Pollak

ABOVE RIGHT: Photo of Maximilian Pollak

University's Sterling Memorial Library (a place in which I have surely spent thousands of hours of my life) to find a book that had sat on dusty shelves for years all about a family member we never knew we had, it was an exhilarating and paradoxical moment. The final confirmation, from my perspective, of the relationship between "famous Ludwig" and "our Max" came in those very diaries when Ludwig records a visit to him in Rome by his brother Max! I subsequently corresponded with Dr. Guldan and wish to acknowledge her correspondence and publications as the source of much of what I will describe below. Delighted to find in Jeanette an indirect survivor of Pollak, Dr. Guldan generously sent us a copy of the Pollak diary book she had annotated and edited.[3]

The Prague that Ludwig Pollak (and his siblings) were born into was then part of the heavily Jewish "Galicia" province of the Austro-Hungarian empire. Based on US Ellis Island records that often list nationality as "Austrian," many Jews today think of their ancestry as being "Austrian" (with all the dreams of Viennese nobility-associated status and Sacher tortes that might convey in their minds) but the humbler reality for most is that their ancestors were most likely from lands that today we would think of as the Czech Republic, or Poland, or Ukraine, for example. Nonetheless, the Habsburg monarchy and Austrian Empire had a real and worldly influence on the lands it commanded.

In Prague Ludwig Pollak studied art history and classical archaeology. From there he moved to Vienna, where he eventually received a doctorate in the field. Because Rome was THE place to be for sculpture, he moved to Rome in 1893, Ph.D. in hand. There his expert eye and his commercial talent soon made him one of the most highly recommended art-dealers. Perhaps his greatest claim to fame came in 1906 when he found in a Rome stonecutter's yard an arm of a presumed 2,000-year-old statue. Making a discovery that would merit a life's glory for any art

Laocoön and His Sons sculpture

꙰

scholar, Pollak successfully identified the source of that piece of stone. He then donated to the Vatican what he had identified to be part of the missing marble right arm of the world-renowned statue of *Laocoön and His Sons*. This monumental sculpture was said to have greatly influenced the young Michelangelo when it was first found in Rome exactly four hundred years before Pollak's find. Another thesis has it that the statue was actually a forgery made by Michelangelo himself about 1506.[4] Whatever its provenance, that statue grouping has been displayed in the Vatican for most of the four centuries since Pope Julius II acquired it and had it brought there. Soon after Pollak's gift, Pope Pius X publicly recognized his immense scholarly and generous contribution by awarding him the title of Commendator of the Gregorian Order, a form of knighthood. Pollak is the first known Jew in history to receive this honor.

With Pollak's reputation in sculpture surely cemented by the papal honor, all the best collectors, including America's John Pierpont Morgan and France's Edmond de Rothschild, bought through him or consulted with him. He served as imperial advisor on sculpture to Emperor Franz Joseph of Austria. His work for the Museo Barracco was of special importance, as he helped Count Giovanni Barracco edit a new catalogue for the collection, and later, at Barracco's request, became its first director in 1914 after Barracco's death.[5] Other famous collectors in Rome had Pollak write the catalogues for their collections. As he was himself an art-dealer, many famous statues went through his hands: the *Athena* of Myron for Frankfurt, *Hermes Odeschalcht* for Copenhagen and the *Vulneratus deficiens* for the Metropolitan Museum of Art in New York. Today, when my wife and I visit that museum, we turn left from the main entryway, and walk down the Greek and Roman Art hall to check on that "Wounded Warrior."

Vulneratus deficiens
(Wounded Warrior) statue
≈

Later, when Italy and Germany signed in 1938 a "Pact of Steel" to form a military alliance, Ludwig Pollak must have shuddered. Historian Guldan noted that some of Pollak's non-Jewish friends and acquaintances avoided him for fear of spies because it was known that he was vocal with his opinions that were critical of Fascism and Naziism. Some of his writings reflect his dismay as a Jew over the stripping of civil rights in Italy that had once been so valued by him.

The last chapter of Ludwig's life reads like a scene from a spy novel or a Hollywood movie: almost a reverse *The Monuments' Men* writ true. After the imprisonment of Benito Mussolini on July 25, 1943 and the subsequent invasion of Italy by German forces in September, 1943, the SS arrived in Italy to pursue the same anti-Jewish processes of murder that they were carrying out elsewhere in Europe. Among the Germans arriving in Rome was William Mohnen, ostensibly a Luftwaffe attaché at the German Embassy in Rome, and one of the Germans who later were investigated by the US "Roberts Commission" that led the authentic "Monuments Men."[6] Once owner of a bicycle and motorcycle business in Mannheim, Germany, Mohnen forged a military career that led him to become something of an art expert belonging to a department of the German occupation assigned to procure valuable works of art from Germany's conquered lands on behalf of Luftwaffe Commander Hermann Göring. Mohnen's arrival in Rome followed a two-year tour of likely similar duty in Paris. In Rome he was also assigned to support diplomatic relations with the Vatican. Whether Mohnen thought well of Pollak from a previous encounter in the rarefied art history world or simply by reputation is unclear, but, for whatever reason, Mohnen apparently took an interest in saving Pollak from the impending German danger.

As the Germans planned to implement their "Final Solution" in Rome by rounding up its Jews on October 16, 1943, Mohnen reached out to Pollak, just a few hours beforehand to warn him. Using his SS and Vatican contacts, Mohnen along with art historian Wolfgang Fritz Volbach secretly came to Pollak and offered to have Pollak arrested with his family "in a safe manner" and immediately transported to protection in the heart of Rome at the Vatican. Mohnen and Volbach warned Pollak that without such sanctuary, the Gestapo they would face would be brutal. Some speculated that conversion to Catholicism might well have been a mandatory part of the offer, but that element is not proven.

For whatever reason lost to history, along with the stories of millions of other lives snuffed out in that dark chapter of our world, Pollak turned Mohnen and his colleague down. He must have been disillusioned by the dark turn in what had been civilization. Even the highest echelons of society were at the mercy of the biological racism that the Nazis promulgated and that Germany enforced. The now seventy-five-year-old Pollak had seen the loss of his daughter Angela to a serious chronic illness the year before. His two other children were adults but had some disabilities that left them weak and unemployed. His wife was chronically ill and dependent on difficult-to-obtain Danish insulin. The Barracco museum that he had been charged with curating had been demolished in 1938 due to urban renewal demands and its artworks moved to a warehouse. One can speculate that perhaps the combination of all these personal challenges in the face of the impending loss of his entire career and possessions left him without the resilience to seek refuge. In October, 1943 he surely knew that two of his three siblings had died of natural causes before the war, and the third (Bertha, at Terezin) was likely already dead or about to be murdered herself. A depressed resignation would have been understandable. Historian Guldan wondered whether an ingrained optimism or overestimation of his relationship with influential Italian authorities and foreign embassy circles might have betrayed his judgment.[7]

We will never know.

In the early morning of October 16, 1943—what became infamous as *sabata nero* (black Saturday)—Ludwig Pollak was arrested by the SS and was never heard from again. Along with his wife, son, and daughter and 1,000 other members of the Jewish community of Rome, Pollak was sent on one train two days later to the death camp at Auschwitz-Birkenau where they perished. If Pollak had made it alive on the five-day trip to that place of infamy, at age seventy-five he surely would have been among the majority immediately selected for the gas chamber.

I have become convinced of the power of William Faulkner's quotation "The past is never dead. It's not even past."[8] So in our family this hitherto unknown-to-us great uncle of my wife's, Ludwig Pollak, lives on at our annual Passover *Seder* in a way that what began as a genealogical hunt could never have foreshadowed. What does Ludwig Pollak's tragic tale have to do with the Passover celebration? Another Ludwig Pollak link from Google took me to a remarkable book that now links Pollak from his birthplace in Prague to his life in Rome and now to New York City. According to online records, after the Second World War, a surviving sister-in-law of Pollak (Margaret Sussman Nicod, from his wife's family) fulfilled a promise he had apparently made to his friend Rabbi David Prato, a former Chief Rabbi of Rome who moved to Jerusalem in 1939 after Mussolini adopted an anti-Jewish policy. One of Pollak's art treasures that survived the war was an illuminated medieval manuscript *Haggadah* (Passover *Seder* song and prayer book) thought to date to Spain from about the year 1300. It is considered one of the two oldest surviving illuminated *Haggadahs* in existence. By 1617 it was in Italy and its provenance over the next 300 years is unknown. Ludwig Pollak had acquired the manuscript in 1908 and considered this purchase a great success. The sister-in-law gave the *Haggadah* to

Rabbi Prato's surviving son Jeonathan in the early 1950s.[9] The younger Prato later sold the volume to the Jewish Theological Seminary (JTS) in New York, where it would be preserved and made available for scholarly access as one of the treasures of its rare book collection.

As a distant relative (and only by marriage) of Ludwig Pollak, I can quibble with the *Haggadah's* today being advertised as the "Prato" *Haggadah*, when the correct provenance of the volume reflects a gift to Rabbi Prato made by the estate of a Shoah victim, and then sold to JTS. In my mind, a more proper designation would be to call it the "Pollak" *Haggadah*, in memory of the tragic end of its pre-war owner. But aside from my petty complaint, I think all the surviving grandnieces and grandnephews of Ludwig Pollak are grateful to see the volume in the protective care of JTS.

As this was written in 2018, the *Haggadah* was on loan from JTS to The Cloisters of the Metropolitan Museum of Art in New York, where it is on display for the general public. Some pages from the volume can be viewed digitally at no cost over the internet. And, for those with the inclination to own their own personal copy of the volume, collector's edition facsimile volumes were produced with gold leaf illumination as in the original and leather board binding and parchment-like leaves. Courtesy of David Kraemer, Professor and Director of the Library at JTS, I was able to surprise Jeanette with a Friday morning visit to JTS right before Passover several years ago. Professor Kraemer then permitted us to have a private audience with the original *Haggadah*, and enjoy, for a moment, a living page of the family history. At our Seders each year, we bring out our own facsimile of the "Pollak *Haggadah*" so all in attendance can celebrate the survival of the Passover quest for identity and freedom despite the challenges of the past.

הַמָּקוֹם בָּרוּךְ הוּא בָּרוּךְ
שֶׁנָּתַן תּוֹרָה לְיִשְׂרָאֵל בָּרוּךְ
הוּא כְּנֶגֶד אַרְבָּעָה בָנִים
דִּבְּרָה תוֹרָה אֶחָד חָכָם
וְאֶחָד רָשָׁע וְאֶחָד תָּם
וְאֶחָד שֶׁאֵינוֹ יוֹדֵעַ לִשְׁאֹל

ABOVE AND OPPOSITE: Pages from Ludwig Pollak's Haggadah

Chapter 5

❧ THE WEDDING PHOTO ❧

One of Jeanette's great-grandmothers was Fella Leiser. Fella's father Hermann Leiser, in partnership with Julius Klausner (husband of Fella's sister Dora), founded the Leiser Shoe company that originated in Germany and later expanded through much of Europe. Leiser Shoes was essentially the family business (with various subsidiaries and spin-offs) for a large extended family of Leisers, Klausners and their relatives. As with so many genealogical explorations, connecting the names and dates of those relatives led me to a breathtaking collection of stories, all drawing from one picture. That "wedding photo" is the subject of this chapter.

Jeanette had been led to believe that her mother's family was of German background. Behind the myth, however, I found that the story of Leiser Shoes, to use a common refrain, began with humble origins. In the

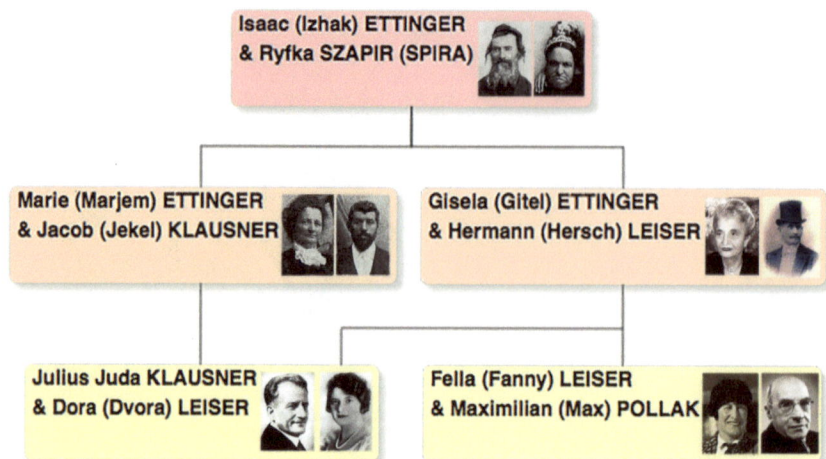

Ettinger family tree

middle-size city in southern Poland of Tarnów, about one hour by car, or one day by horse, from majestic Kraków, a twenty-two-year-old resident named Hermann Leiser married a sixteen-year-old named Gisela Ettinger in 1881. Nine months and two weeks after their wedding date, they moved to Berlin after the birth of their first daughter Dora (registered as Debora). Hermann was the youngest child I know of from about eleven children born to his parents Bezallel and Dwora. (Not all survived past childhood.) To my knowledge, Gisela was the thirteenth child born in her Ettinger family of origin. (About nine others were born afterward.) Gisela was eager to leave home early and her mother supported the move. Hermann came from a reputable but very poor family. Against the will of Gisela's father, her mother forged his signature on a matchmaker's contract to affiance Gisela to Hermann. Once the document became public, Gisela's father had no honorable choice but to acquiesce and provide initial support for the young woman's journey in life.[1]

With so many children underfoot at their respective homes, one can imagine Hermann's and Gisela's parents each encouraging them that their best economic opportunities might come by leaving Tarnów and moving to the newly unified (as of 1871) capital of the German Empire. As a growing capital, in the 1870s alone the Berlin city population increased some 40 percent from about 800,000 to about 1.1 million. Expanding cities usually mean expanding business. Likely anticipating opportunity, Hermann and Gisela made the leap 370 miles northwest from Tarnów to Berlin. There, Hermann set up shop in Berlin as an egg peddler, hawking imported eggs from his home province of Galicia—the Austrian empire's region then encompassing much of today's Southern Poland and Western Ukraine. The business barely made a profit. The family's furniture built of egg boxes were flimsy and symbolized their precarious status. A significant number of eggs rotted in the warm weather or were broken in transit to Berlin. But they were cheaper than local eggs, enabling the business to stay afloat and not crack under the pressure.

Hermann's wisest business decision, however, was to turn his egg crates into shoe boxes. After Hermann had been selling eggs for about a decade, Hermann's seventeen-year-old nephew Julius Klausner, originally from Tarnów also, convinced his uncle to enter the shoe business and partner together to found Leiser's *Schuwarenhaus* in Berlin in 1891. A neophyte, Julius quickly failed as a wholesale shoe dealer. Rebounding from an initial defeat, however, Julius took notice of American department store sale techniques and refashioned Leiser Shoes as a direct-to-consumer store with low, fixed prices, as opposed to market/peddler style haggling that had been traditional. Within a few years Leiser Shoes became Berlin's biggest shoe store and the uncle and nephew opened a nationwide network of branches. In 1899 Julius married Gisela and Hermann's daughter Dora Leiser (therefore his first cousin), interlocking a personal and business relationship, as Dora

The first Leiser shoe store, at Oranienßtrasse 39, Berlin. The man in the center is
Julius Klausner, with his wife Dora near him (circa 1900).

ॐ

had been his first saleswoman. Hermann then retired and allowed
the young couple to manage and take over the business. An energetic
executive, Julius engaged his employees to have successful and healthy
lives by eating what we would today call organic foods and by leading employee exercise sessions. Under Julius's and Dora's direction, the
company mastered sales of gloves, scarves and silk stockings. Diversi-
fying its factories and subsidiaries, Leiser Shoes grew to be the largest
shoe chain in Europe.

The fate of Leiser Shoes under the Nazi regime and afterward is
not dissimilar to that of other German-Jewish companies of the era.
Under German pressure, Julius Klausner gradually sold off most of the
company to German interests. Eventually, Germans confiscated the rest.

Leiser Shoe truck bearing company logo (1931)

I had first started trying to learn about the Klausners because of obscure family lore that my wife Jeanette's Leiser ancestors had once been founders or co-founders of Leiser shoes. But beyond the name, no one still alive knew exactly who or what the connection had been. I had been stymied in trying to find evidence of the birth record of the birth of Dora and Fella's mother (and Jeanette's great-grandmother) Gisela. Despite there being indexes online of the birth of over fifteen children born to Isak Ettinger and his wife Ryfka of Tarnów, there was no evidence of a Gisela.

Finding Tarnów Jewish genealogical records, indeed all Polish genealogical records, is easier than for many countries due to the heroic work of Stanley Diamond, Harvard MBA-graduate turned genealogist, whose leadership of JRI-Poland, the Jewish Records Index-Poland database has led to the online indexing of millions of Jewish genealogical records from Poland. The Polish State Archives placement of many older records themselves online has made this task even easier. Yet I could find no Gisela Ettinger born in Tarnów that I could definitively link to the presumed parents of Isak and Ryfka. Online indexes are far from perfect, and even original records are incomplete, as, especially in the nineteenth century, it was not unusual for people to be less than fully compliant or timely in registering births. Eventually, by tracking down copies of the original birth records for each of Isak's and Rebecca's recorded children, I was able to determine that in fact Gisela had been recorded in the Tarnów registries as being born on August 11, 1864. What had caused the confusion was that the nineteenth century Polish clerk had initially recorded her name incorrectly as "Reisel" and the twentieth century online index transcriber had mistakenly misread the record and typed that the name was later changed to "Oijel" rather than "Gitel," a Yiddish equivalent for the German name Gisela. Two mistakes in two different centuries had made the search harder!

Before I could confirm that, however, I found my way to Be'er Sheva, on the northern edge of Israel's Negev desert. In chapter one of this book I mentioned my contact with tombstone text expert Yocheved Klausner. Her husband Yehuda Klausner, Ph.D., former visiting professor of civil engineering at Princeton University and accomplished genealogist, helped us find Gisela's descendants. The two Klausners had retired to the arid climate of Be'er Sheva, where they welcomed Jeanette and me to explore Ettinger and Klausner family history with them. Yehuda Klausner's own genealogical searches had begun with his trying to determine his own family origins. By the time we met in early 2010, he had found over twenty different Jewish Klausner families worldwide, none of whom, much to his disappointment, were his own forebears. Nonetheless, he is a meticulous researcher, had assembled family trees of thousands of Klausners and their relatives, and was happy to share his learning. With only a bit of work, he was able to search his computer files for the Ettinger family that married a Klausner, and he rapidly and kindly supplied us with Ettinger connections that would have otherwise taken me years to find.

One of the first paths that Yehuda Klausner suggested was to search for the surviving grandchildren of Julius Klausner and Dora Ettinger's three daughters. Facebook had not yet saturated the world in 2010, so it was harder then than it is today to find distant relatives. But a Google search led me to Noa Venezian, granddaughter of Julius and Dora's daughter Margot Klausner. Jeanette's parents had met Margot, as

Mooly, Noa, and Dan (*left to right*) at Noa's home (2010)

she had moved to Palestine before World War II and she later achieved significant public recognition for founding in 1949 the Herzliyah Film Studios that would become Israel's premier television and film producer. Margot was also a principal founder of the famous *Habimah* Theater in Israel. But the family connection to Margot's family had faded over time. Noa and her lovely family invited Jeanette and me to dinner at their home in the peaceful northern town of Hosha'ya in Israel. Joining us was her younger sister Mooly. We sat by the computer figuring out how our families were related.

Mooly Landesman and her husband Zlil are documentary film-makers, whose recent work "Saga of a Photo" is a personal biography of Margot Klausner. In the course of the evening, Mooly shared with us an amazing photograph that was the starting point for the described film biography, and for me the source of the inquiry that forms this chapter.

Mooly had recently found the photograph amongst possessions left behind when her grandmother Margot's sister Käthe Klausner died in Vienna at the astonishing age of 107 in 2009. Our family calls this striking picture "The Wedding Photo."

It is hard not to gasp when looking at this photo. I have since examined this photo hundreds of times and it still brings the same sense of awe back to me. It is a snapshot of an astounding moment in time, and a genealogical treasure. Mooly had recognized that the photo was taken at the wedding of her grandparents Margot Klausner and

OPPOSITE:
Wedding photo of
Margot Klausner and Jacob Rosner,
Hotel Adlon, Berlin (May 20, 1926)

Jacob (Jak) Rosner, on May 20, 1926. Through comparing this photo with photographs from the era, I was later able to prove that the setting was the ballroom of Berlin's Hotel Adlon, one of the most famous hotels in Europe, then and now (today the Adlon Kempinski). The elegant white tie dress of the attendees in the photograph showed this wedding to be the most formal of affairs. Guests might well have been wearing Leiser's own ballroom shoes, as depicted in the postage stamp style advertisement!

Advertising stamp for
Leiser ballroom shoes

The father of the bride, sitting just behind the groom in the photo was Julius Klausner, one of the most successful businessmen in Berlin of his era. The wedding of his daughter Margot surely celebrated the joy they felt. That marriage would collapse within two years, but it produced one child: Miriam, mother of siblings Vered, Noa, Yaakov, and Mooly.

When Mooly and I first saw this photo virtually everyone in the photo was a stranger to us. Yet, knowing there would be family members to be found in that picture, I made it a personal mission to find out, to the extent I could, who were the people in that portrait, and what their stories were. As of this writing, I have identified thirty-three of the seventy-eight people in the photo. Perhaps this book's publication will yield more. But what I found was sometimes extraordinary.

In tragic retrospective, the photographer captured an exuberance and innocence and affluence that would be swept away for most a decade later. I would learn that the people sitting in those chairs were a microcosm of what would befall most of the world Jewish community over the next two decades.

Though this group was certainly not average economically—a few of them extraordinarily wealthy—their fates tell the story of the Shoah. We will never know if this photo was left for decades in a drawer because it represented a failed marriage, or perhaps the tragedies that would befall so many in the photo in so many ways was too much too bear. Of those faces I now recognize, many in the photo would survive the war, many would not. Surely all who lived through the war survived with psychological or physical scars, seen or unseen, and haunted memories, revealed or hidden. Whatever pain the photo symbolically carried, its owner had left it for history to explore.

As I look at the numbered key that Jeanette and I prepared, I lovingly recall a very special woman who helped identify and lead me to so many people in the scene: Lilo (Liselotte) Leiser, born in Berlin in 1919, granddaughter of Hermann Leiser and Gisela (Ettinger) Leiser. Shortly, I will share her unique story in the context of her parents (who appear in the photo). But for now, it is worth recounting how I reached her. Once Mooly shared the photo with me, I wondered if there was someone still alive who might have known some of those depicted. Without a guide, I had imagined I might have had to spend the rest of my life with the overwhelming task of poring through archives around the world. Even that modern miracle of Google, which has helped this task in countless ways, is not yet up to that challenge.

The task, still uncompleted, was not always easy, but I could not desist from it. While most family members I tried to interview were the most genial and eager to speak with me—a family member by marriage who was interested in their personal and collective story—a few very firmly refused to comment at all. In the absence of their statements I can only guess at what drove their psychology. Understandably marked by the physical and psychological trauma of the war years, a few of the children and grandchildren of those in the photo stopped identifying themselves as Jews in the postwar years. Perhaps my asking about family history risked taking them to a dark corner of their past they preferred not to explore. For some, their refusal might have reflected typical family rivalries, exacerbated by a world-shaking war. This was a very, very large family and surely the jealousies as ancient as Cain and Abel that occur within families (indeed within any human group) still percolated. Perhaps there was some pre-war intra-family resentment that still carried force ninety years after the photo was taken? Certainly not everyone in the family or photo was wealthy or successful—before the war or after. I do know that a few were bitter or jealous that they did not receive postwar monies they felt they deserved. Certainly not everyone in the family or photo suffered the same during the time and aftermath of the war and some quietly resented not receiving more assistance from others in the family during the war years and after the war. I am sure each had their own reasons. Fortunately, it took only one amazing woman to give broader clarity to the photo. From there, other doors opened.

Jeanette's uncle Peter (né Taubenschlag) Townsend had told me a few years before about Lilo (née Leiser) Nesviginsky, a ninety or so-year-old first cousin of his mother Edith. He reported that Lilo (whose formal name was Liselotte) would frequently call him at home in Syracuse, New York from her apartment in Buenos Aires, Argentina. For him, memories of the Nazi-era Berlin that he had been born into and narrowly escaped from as a child were more of an annoyance than an interest. But he was happy to share the link to Lilo with me. I jumped on this opportunity, and, with Skype having just made the cost of international calls most affordable, as soon as I had a copy of the photo, I reached out to Lilo, whom I hoped might be my guide. Widowed since 2005, her son Jorge having moved to Canada years before that, Lilo was living alone in Buenos Aires, and we became best phone-friends. It was a good match, as she loved to talk about the long-gone past, and I was interested in hearing her stories. She still remembered the times long gone by, far better she said, as is common at that age, than events of the previous day. In 1926, at age seven, Lilo had been too young to attend her cousin Margot's wedding, but she had known a good number of the guests and she still remembered them years later. She could sometimes offer critical clues about their fate that led me to some of their descendants. Lilo passed away three years later at age ninety-four in 2013, marveling each time that I spoke to her over the miracle of her surviving the Shoah and living to such a ripe age. To the day of this writing, when, as happens often, I come across written documents that confirm family relationships and identities that give proof to Lilo's memories, I remain in awe at her accurate recollections.

With Lilo's specific help in some cases, and with her inspiration in so many others, I was able to assemble the partial key to the photo below. Even this partial list of names is overwhelming, and I would encourage the reader not to let him or herself become similarly overwhelmed by mastering the individual names. Yet I include all that I do know because everyone has a history and this photo opens the door to events that deserve to be recalled even as the names slip from our memory.

1. **Margot Klausner**, the bride

2. **Jak Rosner**, the groom

3. **Friederike (Fanny) (née Klausner) Hulles**, sister of Julius Klausner

4. **Meyer Hulles**, husband of Fanny Hulles

5. **Dora (née Leiser) Klausner**, wife of Julius Klausner, mother of bride Margot Klausner

6. **Oscar Rosner**, father of groom Jacob Rosner and husband of Sydonie

7. **Sydonie Rosner**, mother of groom Jacob Rosner and wife of Oscar

8. **Julius Klausner**, husband of Dora Klausner, father of bride Margot Klausner

9. **Gisela (née Ettinger) Lichtmann**, former widow of Hermann Leiser, wife of Benno Lichtmann, mother of Dora and Fella Leiser, grandmother of bride Margot Klausner

10. **Ilse Klausner**, daughter of Julius and Dora

11. **Max Pollak**, husband of Fella Leiser and son-in-law of Gisela Lichtmann

12. **Max Leiser**, father of Lilo and brother of Dora, Fella and his twin Joseph

13. **Lilli (née Arenstein) Blumenstein**, daughter of Ida (Tsherne) Leiser and second cousin of bride Margot

14. **Margarethe (Grethe) (née Sieger) Hauptmann**, wife of Harry Hauptmann, sister of Ella (née Sieger) Klausner

15. **Elly Rose (née Oppenheim) Leiser**, mother of Lilo and wife of Max Leiser

16. **Ella (née Sieger) Klausner**, wife of Otto Klausner, sister of Margarethe Hauptmann

17. **Elsa Rosner**, sister of groom Jacob Rosner

19. **Rosie (née Reichman) Leiser**, married to Joseph

20. **Joseph Leiser**, brother of Dora, Fella and his twin Max

21. **Ida (Tsherne) (née Leiser) Arenstein**, mother of Lilli Blumenstein and first cousin of Dora Klausner

22. **Sabina Klausner**, sister of Julius Klausner and aunt of bride Margot

24. **Johanna Perl Ettinger**, wife of Salomon Ettinger

25. Possibly, **Ludwig Pollak**, (see previous chapter) brother of Max Pollak

26. **Wilhelm Klausner**, brother of Julius Klausner

31. **Benno Lichtmann**, second husband of Gisela (following the death of Hermann Leiser)

33. **Salomon Ettinger**, brother of Gisela Lichtmann

34. **Horst Wilhelm Klausner**, son of Heinrich Klausner and first cousin of bride Margot

35. **Heinrich Klausner**, brother of Julius Klausner, nephew of Gisela Lichtmann, and uncle of bride Margot

38. **Heinrich Arenstein**, husband of Ida Arenstein

39. **Max Blumenstein**, husband of Lilli Arenstein

50. **Alice Ettinger**, daughter of Salomon Ettinger and niece of Gisela Lichtmann

51. **Edith Pollak**, daughter of Max Pollak and Fella Leiser and first cousin of bride Margot

58. **Ludwig Klausner**, brother of Julius Klausner and nephew of Gisela Lichtmann

75. **Paula (née Ettinger) Roemer**, daughter of Salomon and Johanna and niece of Gisela Lichtmann, wife of Gerhard Roemer

76. **Gerhard Roemer**, husband of Paula Ettinger.

Not yet identified: 18, 23, 27-30, 32, 36-37, 40-49, 52-57, 59-74, 77-78.

＊　＊　＊

I have already recounted the essentials of Margot's later accomplishments and life in Palestine and Israel. Below are the most poignant of the histories I have found for some of those in the photo. The numbers in parentheses after people's names refer to their location in the wedding photo above. The remaining accounts that I found appear in Appendix One.

✦ Julius Klausner (8) and Dora (née Leiser) Klausner (5): Though Leiser Shoes was gradually sold under duress to Nazi sympathizers, Julius and Dora Klausner remained in Berlin, thinking their extraordinary past success and influence would protect them. Even the events of spring 1933 were insufficient to move them to escape. Though Jews made up less than one percent of the total German population, they were the primary scapegoat of the Nazi rise to power. On April 1, the Nazi leadership, acting through their SA and SS members, began a nationwide boycott of Jewish-owned businesses, and blamed Jews for anti-German tone in the international press. At one Leiser factory, one exceptionally-well compensated non-Jewish employee ("Gizzy") stood outside and yelled "Juden, raus" to demand the Jews leave the building. Other non-Jewish factory workers turned on the Jewish employees and joined the chants. Warning posters were placed on the windows of Leiser shops.[2] Julius soon began to sell portions of his business in order to mitigate his losses on the day when he would later be forced to sell the entire business, but dearly held on to a remaining 25 percent of the business despite Nazi coercion. In order to get passports and documents that would allow Julius and his wife eventually to leave Germany, Julius and Dora were forced to pay over 3.5 million Reichsmarks (worth about 1.5 million US dollars in the currency of the era).[3] A fortune by any account, but worth every *pfennig* to save their lives. Before becoming mass murderers, the German government exercised mass extortion. When Dora and Julius received news in late 1937 from Dora's sister-in-law Rosie Leiser that the Germans planned to arrest Julius, the couple fled Germany the same day: Julius by plane to Amsterdam, and Dora by train to Switzerland, from where she made her way to Holland. Julius and Dora stayed in Holland at least through April 1939, and then travelled to Buenos Aires, Argentina before Germany invaded Holland.[4]

After the war, 50 percent ownership of Julius's Leiser Shoe firm was returned to him as compensation for his losses. He never again managed the business. The other half remained with Dietrich Bahner, the German who had bought the bulk of the company before the war. Julius died in 1950 at age seventy-six in Buenos Aires. Despite the trauma their adopted homeland of Germany had imposed on them, Julius and Dora somehow still maintained close ties to Berlin. Dora frequently returned there after Julius's death to supervise the family business and she died there in 1959. Following her death, Julius's remains were transferred next to hers in Berlin's Charlottenburg Jewish cemetery. After Dora moved out of her Buenos Aires apartment, her niece Lilo (who was so helpful to me) moved in and happily lived amidst the memories of Julius and Dora. Postwar Leiser Shoes, under non-Klausner management, had mixed success, including at least one episode of bankruptcy, but its prominent logo and sales across Germany and parts of Europe continue to this day. The neon lights of Leiser still dominate the scene on Berlin's Tauentzienstraße, across the street from the famed KaDeWe department store. As in the photo I took of my daughter Amalyah in that exact location, great-great-grandchildren of Hermann Leiser and other distant relatives of Julius and Dora Klausner still visit on rare occasions to imagine a charmed past. Few descendants or passersby realize it is the same site where history was once written and an anti-Jewish boycott (as shown below) had once taken place.

ABOVE: Boycott of Leiser Shoe store on Tauentzienstraße, Berlin (March, 1933)

LEFT: Amalyah Oren in front of Tauentzienstraße Leiser Shoe Store, Berlin (Nov. 9, 2010)

✦ MAX (12) AND ELLY LEISER (15) AND DAUGHTER LILO:

A champion springboard diver during his Berlin youth, Max, one of two sons of Hermann and Gisela Leiser, later worked for the family shoe business in Germany. Although they felt the sting of Germany's biological racism at least as early as 1933 when their daughter Lilo (my irreplaceable source) was told as a fourteen-year-old that, as a Jew, she was to be expelled from her high school, it took a few years, as conditions for Jews deteriorated, for Max and Elly to develop an escape plan. By paying a small fortune that they hoped might buy them life, Max and Elly were able to procure Costa Rican passports from Baron Hermann Rautenberg, an Austrian and ostensibly-former Nazi who served as Consul General from Costa Rica to Berlin during the 1930s. This payment may well have been one of many that Rautenberg took in such manner from desperate victims of the Germans.[5] Along with a number of family members yearning to find safety amidst the Nazi threat, Max and Elly decided to move to Amsterdam in 1938, where Max was one of the owners of the Leiser family-controlled "Huff" shoe business. Strip-searched by the SS (to prevent illegal export of valuables) before leaving Berlin, the family was then permitted to fly to Amsterdam. A more humane connection in Amsterdam proved useful. Alberto Enrique Grimoldi, a non-Jewish Argentinian businessman Lilo vividly remembered who had visited Max and Elly's stores to learn innovative sales techniques, allowed them to transfer legal ownership of the Amsterdam business to him with a verbal promise that he would protect their financial interests until the day would come when they could safely reclaim them. In May 1940, beginning with *Luftwaffe* bombing raids, the German military invaded the Netherlands. Thereafter, often with the cooperation of Dutch authorities, they deported most of the country's Jews to German-built and operated concentration and death camps. On the night of the invasion, Lilo's aunt Rosie (19) Leiser chartered a boat to take Max, Elly, and Lilo from Holland to safety in England and sent a taxi to pick them up in Amsterdam and bring them to the harbor. But, as Lilo recalled, two friends of the family who were staying at the same location in Amsterdam, "stole" the chartered taxi to make their escape from the German peril. Lilo's family was left behind as alternate prey. Despite holding the Costa Rican passports, the family was soon arrested and deported to the Westerbork transit camp in the German-occupied Netherlands. This was the same site where Anne Frank would later be transported before her final deportation to Auschwitz.

Up until Lilo's ninety-fifth and last year of life, her recollection of Westerbork was detailed and unsparing. Men and women were separated, assigned to sleep in barn-like conditions on straw mattresses and multi-level iron bunks. Secretly, she fashioned a horsehair-stuffed pillow that she retained through her entire life as a souvenir of her encounter with the bloody edge of the Shoah. She was assigned to work as a cook in the camp hospital. By virtue of the confirmation of the authenticity of the family's Costa Rican passports, however, in 1944, rather than being deported to Auschwitz (as was Anne Frank's destiny later that year), Max, Elly, and Lilo were instead moved to a refugee camp in La Bourboule, France. Soon after, their freedom was assured when the Allied forces invaded the north coast of France at Normandy.

After the war they moved to Uruguay and then, with the aid of their friend Grimoldi, were able to immigrate to Argentina in 1948. Grimoldi had apparently told the Juan Perón government that Max's technical knowledge of the footwear business was critical to Grimoldi's plans to develop his own shoe business in Argentina. Further, Grimoldi acted as the family's personal sponsor and guarantor of the family's fiscal stability to the Argentinian government. To his honor and everlasting credit, after these Leisers settled in Argentina, Grimoldi returned to them the monies and the financial equivalent of all the assets of the family business in Holland that had been left under his management. And the family could build new lives.

✦ Rosie (19) and Josef Leiser (20):

Josef Leiser was Lilo's uncle and the brother of Lilo's father Max. Identical twin sons of Gisela and Hermann Leiser, Josef and Max had been born back in Tarnów before the family moved to Berlin. Their son Herman (named after his grandfather Hermann) was born in 1920, six years prior to the wedding photo. Blond and blue-eyed, the young Herman later recalled an idyllic life, including the odd recollection of having once being invited to join the SS, who assumed he was Aryan and a Nazi.[6] After the German-inspired violence and boycotts of 1933, Rosie and Josef's family fled to Switzerland for a brief time. Still feeling an inexorable pull of their adopted German homeland, they later decided to return to Berlin because it was, after all was said and done, their home, and they thought the "Hitler phase" for Germany would pass. But it did not pass without terrible consequences. As noted above, late in 1937 Rosie learned from a friend in the Gestapo that the Germans planned to arrest Julius Klausner the next day. Rosie ran over to the Klausner villa a few blocks away in Berlin and alerted her sister-in-law Dora and Dora's husband Julius about the impending danger. Soon after, Rosie and Josef themselves were arrested and imprisoned for a number of weeks in Berlin. After release (and presumably after payment of a significant sum) they and their children fled Germany to Amsterdam. With the invasion of Holland by Germany in May 1940, Rosie knew her family would no longer be safe there. Learning that Jews trying to escape to England were being arrested at harbors or returned to Amsterdam, Rosie organized taxis to take her family to the harbor in the middle of the night. There she found a small fishing boat whose master was willing to risk taking them on a stormy night through the mine-strewn waters to England. Lowering her elderly parents into the boat by rope, and then boarding with her husband and children, she led them to safety. They eventually made their way to Canada and later to New York City. Rosie died young of cancer in 1943 at age forty-five.

✦ HEINRICH (38) AND IDA (NÉE LEISER) ARENSTEIN (21), MAX (39) AND LILLI (13) (NÉE ARENSTEIN) BLUMENSTEIN:

In the course of Google-surfing for Leisers, aided by Lilo's names, I found yet a new lead when I came across the name of Ralph Blumenstein, then living in Forest Hills, Queens, New York City. On a cold December day in 2011, then eighty-four-year-old Ralph and his wife Trudy warmly welcomed us to their apartment. We talked about Leiser shoes, for which his father Max (who had married his mother Lilli, a Leiser cousin) had once

Ralph Blumenstein,
Queens, New York
(Dec. 26, 2011)

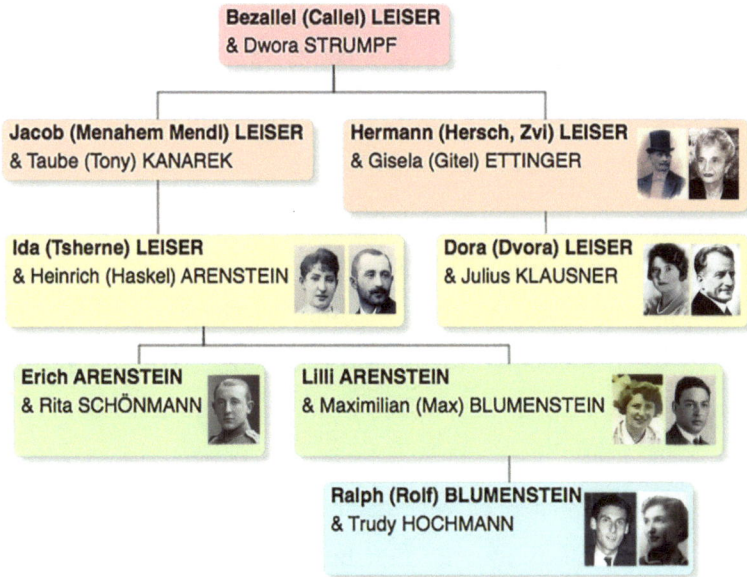

Ralph Blumenstein family tree

ॐ

worked. Max had died of natural causes well before World War II, and Ralph's family lore had it (mistakenly) that his ancestors had founded Leiser Shoes. Ralph studied the wedding photo with great interest. In private, out of Trudy's earshot, he told us an account that still shakes me when I think about it. The wedding photo had been taken eighty-five years earlier, a full year before his birth, and he had never seen it before. Yet, as seen in the photo at left from that day, he could easily recognize his parents and grandparents in attendance.

His grandmother Ida (born Tsherne Leiser, in Tarnów) was a first cousin of Dora Klausner, mother of the bride. Ida and her husband Heinrich (born Haskel in Warsaw) were living in Berlin at the time of the 1926 wedding. Though many of the people in the wedding photo survived the Shoah, Ida and Heinrich Arenstein did not, and their descendants suffered severely as well. Escaping in parallel with others of the family to what they hoped would be safety in Amsterdam, they, too, came under the threat of arrest and deportation to near-certain death after the Germans invaded Holland. Heinrich, then age seventy-seven, committed suicide in Amsterdam on October 5, 1942 when he knew that arrest by German police was imminent. Ida was arrested around that same time and deported to the Sobibór death camp in occupied Poland. She was murdered there on July twenty-third the next year. Their son Erich spent part of the war in Nice, France, but was later arrested as well. On February 10, 1944 he was deported from Drancy concentration camp, France to Auschwitz, where he perished. His wife was likely murdered there as well. Ida and Heinrich's daughter Lilli had married Rudolf Jolles after her first husband Max Blumenstein died young. Together with husband Rudolf and her two sons Ralph and Klaus, Lilli spent the first half of the war hiding in Amsterdam. The second half was what still makes me shudder.

When Ralph's wife Trudy stepped into the kitchen to make us coffee, Ralph quietly volunteered a report to Jeanette and me that he said he had never told his children, not having wanted them to live with the psychological burden of knowing his full wartime experience. In 2017, before completing this chapter, I telephoned Trudy, a Shoah survivor who had experienced severe trauma and losses herself during the war and asked her what she had known about Ralph's wartime experiences. Despite their love and their fifty-five years together as a married couple, she explained that it was not her place to ask him about that terrible chapter in his life and she had never done so. She had thought, as Ralph had described above, that he had spent the entire war in hiding in Holland. Of course, it is not unusual for victims of severe trauma not to discuss their past experiences, so his silence to her and his children on this matter was respected. During our visit Ralph had told us that he had been seriously ill not so long before our visit to him. I don't know if he knew that within months of our visit to his apartment he would die of natural causes at age eighty-four. In the context of seeing the photo of his parents and grandparents from a time long past, and at least an inkling that his remaining time on earth was very limited, Ralph chose to tell us a few remaining details that he did not want to leave unshared forever.

Before Trudy could return with the coffee, Ralph told us that in fact, he, his brother, and his mother had been arrested in Holland and spent the second half of the war in various concentration camps. In one, he recalled, he had been selected for the freezing/hypothermia experiments often associated with Dr. Mengele. In those particularly cruel forms of torture conducted ostensibly to provide data to support the German war effort in the cold of the Eastern Front, concentration camp prisoners might be strapped outside naked in frigid temperatures (as Ralph reported experiencing) with the goal of establishing how long it would take to lower their body temperatures to the point of death or near death. Ralph was grateful to survive but reported carrying with him psychological and physical scars of that torture to that very day. With Trudy returning to the room, he chose to say no more.

After the war, Ralph and his brother, their mother Lilli and their stepfather Rudolf Jolles, made their way to New York. Lilli died in 1996. Ralph died fewer than five months after we met, in May, 2012. Trudy subsequently moved to the Midwest to live near her son and daughter.

✦ Ella and Ludwig Klausner (58):

If there are rays of light that emerge amidst the horrors of the Shoah, some of the brightest ones come from a man named Ludwig Klausner, brother of the bride's father Julius. Lilo recognized him and identified him to me. Most of what I know about Ludwig was shared with me by his step-daughter Magda. I learned of her existence through reading her name in a *New York Times* death notice I found by searching the *Times* website as part of my hunt for information about Ludwig:

> **KLAUSNER—Ludwig**, on March 9, 1964, husband of Rose Hornik
> Klausner, father of Hans Stephen Klausner, stepfather of Mrs. Magda
> Nemlich and Mrs. Lotte Scharfman. Funeral was held Wednesday,
> March 11, 1964.[7]

Although he had died forty-six years before I came across this notice in 2010, finding it led me to hope that one of his children or stepchildren might still be alive, and open up a door to his past. Initially, I was stymied and unable to find a record, living or deceased, of stepdaughters Magda or Lotte. A Google search led me to a 2000 book written by an inspiring rabbi named Aryeh Ben David dedicated to his parents Alan and Magda Nemlich. With Ben David having changed his surname quite remote from Nemlich, in the absence of that dedication phrase, I might still have been looking for Magda today. Seeing her name in print from 2000 gave me hope that she might still be alive just ten years later in 2010. After tracking down Aryeh, he put me in touch with his mother Magda. Fortunately, she was just an hour down the road from us, living with her husband in Westchester, New York, and they cheerfully welcomed Jeanette and me for a visit.

Although I have not yet been able to identify which of the women in the photo (if any) was Ludwig's then-wife Ella (née Leitner) Klausner, the distinctive face of Ludwig Klausner ("Klausi," as Magda called him) was readily identifiable both to Lilo and to Magda. Eleven years younger than father-of-the-bride Julius Klausner, Ludwig had also been born in Tarnów, then Galicia, today Poland. When Ludwig reached the age of twenty-two in 1907, he and Julius expanded the Leiser shoe business from Germany into Austria by co-founding the Austrian Del-Ka shoe company. The Del-Ka name was a playful quasi-anagram taken from the names of Julius and Ludwig's wives **Do**ra and El**la** **K**lausner.

The two Klausner brothers owned about 75 percent of the company and about 8 percent was owned by Ludwig and Julius's sister Fanny (3) (née Klausner). As I gradually learned about the interlocking and sometimes enmeshed ownership of this specific family business, as a model for many of the other family shoe-related businesses, I came to understand how descendants of the original owners would often later come to think that their particular ancestor was "the" rightful or sole owner of the family enterprise, when in fact that ownership might well have just been a partial ownership and might well have been just for a limited point in time before one partner bought another out. In other cases, some of the businesses might have been successful, but only kept afloat by loans meant to be repaid out of future profits. And when the businesses were subsequently and forcibly sold for *pfennigs* on the *Deutsche Mark*, or liquidated entirely without compensation, a recipe for misunderstandings and disappointment were created. In the case of Del-Ka, the firm was also 16 percent was owned by the Creditanstalt-Wiener Bankverein, a bank originally founded by the Rothschild family of Europe.[8] By 1938 this bank had become the largest and most important bank in Austria. Interconnecting the leading personalities of banking and industry in Austria, leading industrialists sat on its board, of which Ludwig was "Director General." The bank by then had also become a major instrument of the Austrian government, which controlled a majority of its shares.

Before the First World War, Del-Ka had expanded to seven stores. Later led entirely by Ludwig, Del-Ka prospered further. It developed major subsidiaries elsewhere in Europe (including Del-Ka in Hungary

Del-Ka advertisement (artist Hans Neumann)

and Slovakia, and Orzel in Poland) and significant interests in other shoe-related production and sales firms. Ludwig himself achieved the heights of Austrian business society and responsibility and served as president of the guild of large commercial enterprises in Austria. Despite the increasing threats towards Jews in nearby Germany, for most of the 1930s, Ludwig saw his success as ensuring his security against any possible danger in his adopted nation of Austria.

The rarefied world that Ludwig and his wife Ella inhabited came crashing down upon them when German troops occupied Austria on March 12, 1938. In a bloodless coup, the next day Hitler proclaimed the *Anschluss* in which Austria became a province of Germany. Viennese citizenry cheered the arrival of the Nazis: some had had already been engaging in anti-Jewish violence and many relished the new German entertainment of forcing Jews to clean the streets with toothbrushes or the like. Across former Austria, confiscation of Jewish assets and expulsions began.[9] Ludwig and Ella spent the next few days debating how to respond to the crisis. Ella was certain the only option was to flee. The fifty-two-year-old Ludwig, at the prime of his life and career, confident that the social and business status he had built up over the prior thirty years would protect him from the turmoil, still believed it was safe to stay. They decided to separate for the moment: Ella would escape by taking a train to Switzerland; Ludwig would stay in Vienna.

Ludwig escorted Ella to the Vienna train station and saw her aboard the train. As the train was departing, Ella looked out the window and saw Ludwig being arrested by Gestapo forces who were beating some of their arrestees and who then loaded Ludwig into a truck that would take him to a police prison. The German captors announced to the world that a group of newly-arrested prisoners, including Ludwig Klausner and Creditanstalt Bank scion Baron Louis de Rothschild had been taken into "protective custody," possibly to be released "as soon as their personal safety could be assured."[10] Such language was a veil for brutality and extortion.

Ludwig Klausner was stunned by his arrest. When I found a book in the dark stacks of Yale's Sterling Memorial Library describing Klausner's own words in that prison, the hindsight of today casts light on the naivety of him and his generation: "What can they intend to do with us? What can they want with me, an entirely unpolitical industrialist?" From the prison block, Ludwig was pulled in for interrogation and returned to his cellmates, sober and informed: "They want my factory . . . 'Aryanizing' it, they call it." He insisted to his interrogators that he first be released before he would settle the financial terms for the confiscation of his factory. Clinging to unrealistic hope, he told his fellow prisoners

Section of Ludwig Klausner's Dachau prisoner registry card

that he thought his release was imminent. Instead he would be sent to a German hell on Earth.[11]

Ludwig and 150 others were taken from the German police prison to the *Westbahnhof*, the Viennese railway station leading to Dachau, the town whose name struck terror in Austria even before it achieved worldwide notoriety. This very first deportation of prisoners from Vienna to Dachau was later nicknamed the *"Prominentransport,"* a German shipment of "VIPs" for immediate oppression. Ludwig was number 34 on the typed list the Gestapo prepared of 151 people designated as priorities for arrest and removal from Vienna that April 1, 1938.[12] This group entered the concentration camp on April 2. Ludwig's Dachau prisoner registry card, noting him as prisoner 13911 appears above.

Most of the group were either Jews or political officials whom the Germans wished to remove as potential obstructions to their control. Dachau was the first concentration camp built in Germany and had been intended to hold political prisoners. Yet, as Gerald Feldman has written

about arrests of leading Jewish industrialists, Dachau was used for mer-
cenary purposes as well:

> The placing of Jewish family owners in Dachau or other concentration
> camps, thereby making them hostages for the surrender of their enter-
> prises and assets, became something of a standard procedure in large
> Aryanizations.[13]

In the case of Ludwig, Dachau was first used to beat him repeatedly
into submission and then to extort his assets. When possible, Ludwig
correctly told his tormenters he was a shoemaker in the hope that his
having a useful skill would lead to better treatment.

I do not know if Ella ever reached Switzerland, but panicked by what
she had observed at the train station, fearful for the fate of her husband,
Ella returned to Vienna to try to secure Ludwig's release. Whatever her
efforts were, they were fruitless. As *The New York Times* soon reported,
"Families of several Jews interned at Dachau . . . received brief printed slips
notifying them of deaths" there. In the same city where Sigmund Freud
had made his name studying hysteria in earlier decades, the international-
ly-known psychoanalyst himself hurried to escape to England while a mass
hysteria of completely understandable origin swept through. Waves of suicides of Jews and some non-German intellectuals broke out in Vienna in
the aftermath of the Anschluss, the Aryanization of Jewish-owned properties suddenly leaving many destitute, severe restrictions and violence that
kept Jews in their homes, and the threats of deportation to be laborers on
"public works projects" throughout the Reich or threats of death.[14] Amidst
these traumas, on May 9, 1938, Ella Klausner took her own life.

While Ludwig remained under arrest in Dachau, a non-Jewish
attorney for the family tried to negotiate the Aryanization of Ludwig's

business on his behalf. The attorney first requested that Klausner himself be brought back to Vienna to conduct the discussions directly. The attorney pointed out that the other Klausner family members holding shares in Del-Ka felt incompetent to direct the company without Ludwig's lead. The co-owning and now Aryanized Creditanstalt bank dismissed the Jewish directors of Del-Ka and began to negotiate to take full ownership of the company.

Almost six months after arriving at Dachau, Ludwig Klausner was transferred to the Buchenwald Concentration Camp just outside of Weimar, Germany. Ludwig's son Hans, who had been running a Del-Ka subsidiary in Budapest, had travelled to England on business in March, 1938 and, taking Göring's warnings to Austrian Jews seriously, decided not to risk returning to Hungary or Austria. Even though he would be considered an "enemy alien" in wartime Britain, it was far safer to be there than on the European mainland. From England Hans was successfully able to bribe Buchenwald camp officials to help procure his father's release. In parallel efforts, Ludwig surrendered his ownership stake in Del-Ka at 40 percent of its value. But, as historian Feldman has noted, the Creditanstalt bank—as if trying to provide assurance that the Jew Klausner not see any reward for his life's labors—reported that Klausner was left penniless after the transaction, as the gains from the share sale were confiscated to pay imposed taxes. The attorney who negotiated the sale of Del-Ka received Klausner's home in Vienna as his fee. Eventually, in 1940, the bank took full ownership of the company. According to Buchenwald files, Ludwig was released on October 28, 1938.

Aided from Britain by his son Hans, Ludwig was able to then escape from Germany to Switzerland and then make his way to Great Britain. A chance encounter at the seaside town of Penarth, Wales with Rosa Eichenwald—a widow (by natural causes) of a former Masonic lodge-mate of Ludwig's in Vienna, mother of two girls, and now a fellow refugee herself—led to a new relationship for the two of them. Taking separate ships to the US in 1940, they reunited in New York, married in 1941, and built a new life in the New York City suburb of White Plains. Ludwig's son Hans survived the war in Australia (to which Britain had later deported the Austrian-born young man as an "enemy alien") and Ludwig's daughter Edith survived the war in the US.

Having lost everything in Europe but his gentle character and his life itself, needing to earn a living in America, since Ludwig knew the shoe business, he opened a "Dr. Scholes" shoe store franchise in White Plains. He lived a modest life thereafter, never regaining his position or wealth. His stepdaughter Magda Nemlich said he never was bitter about not recovering his finances from the Nazi-forced "fire sale" of his shoe business after his imprisonment. Whether or not it was out of respect to his new wife, or out of sorrow about the loss of his first wife Ella, Magda does not recall "Klausi" ever speaking to them of Ella. A man once on top of the Austrian economy took satisfaction during the war in the simple pleasures of life by growing his own "victory garden" in his backyard, and he earned his bread fitting shoes onto customers in his humble shop. His stepdaughters valued his taking on the role of the father they had lost too early. His son-in-law Alan Nemlich, who only met him after the war, described his father-in-law as "kind and wonderful." Ludwig had faced almost all the tribulations of the biblical Job, losing his prosperity and his wife. All the financial wealth he had lost during the war, however, he turned into love in its aftermath. He died at age seventy-eight in 1964. Under new ownership, at the time of this writing, more than twenty-five DELKA shoe stores can still be found in Vienna and all over Austria.

* * *

With all the sad stories from this wedding photo described above and in the endnotes to this chapter, the question is easy to ask about why more of the family, indeed why most of the family, did not abandon Germany and the region until or after peril arrived. The answer is a too familiar one. As we can see in the photos in the family tree on page 104, in one generation—the generation that moved from Galicia (in today's Poland) to Berlin—the family transitioned from devout East European Orthodox to assimilated West European Reform Judaism. Religious devotion was still regular on the High Holy Days each fall and on Passover, when about one hundred members of the family might attend a *seder* together at the home of Julius and Dora Klausner, and Friday night Sabbath dinners were common. Yet, feeling a full part of German life, their Berlin connection was as much part of their self-definition as any other. They had rapidly achieved the heights of economic success, security and confidence. A dark future was unimaginable. They were wrong.

❋   ❋   ❋

✦ HORST WILHELM KLAUSNER (34) AND HEINRICH KLAUSNER (35): I have withheld one account arising from this photo. Of all the people captured in that moment in 1926, no mystery intrigued me more than that of the single young boy in a sailor suit amidst the white tie-dressed adults. That boy deserves a chapter of his own.

Chapter 6

❧ THE BOY IN THE SAILOR SUIT ❧

From the moment I first studied the wedding photo my eye was drawn to the young boy in the sailor suit. Distinct amongst the multitude of the crowd, a child in a child's uniform amidst the fancily-dressed adults in white tie, who was he? What was his story? What presumably close connection to the family might he have had that gave him entrée to a surely fabulous affair? And, in the way that children have of tugging at our heartstrings, what fate awaited him? The look on his face is a serious one. Did that portend his future? At the time of the 1926 wedding, he looked like he would have been about ten years old. If that guess was correct, in 1939, when World War II broke out, he would have been about twenty-three. For months he was nothing more than a face in a crowd; a face whose mystery captured me.

Lilo (the ninety-plus-year-old Shoah-survivor who knew so many of the people depicted in the wedding photo) was the key to opening this door as well. I can imagine trying to find the classbooks from every school in Berlin from the 1920s, if such volumes even exist, and paging through each one hoping to match the boy in the sailor suit to a name. The tedium of the work would have been numbing, and

Horst Klausner
(May 20, 1926)

even if a match existed, I could easily have missed it. And that assumed the boy was from Berlin. If his home had been elsewhere, the task would have been impossible. Fortunately, Lilo made it easy for me.

Studying the photo, taken when Lilo was a seven-year-old, she immediately recalled the boy as her friend (and second cousin) Horst, the son of Julius Klausner's brother Heinrich Klausner. She recalled Horst as medium in size, with brown eyes, and somewhat shy. She recalled that he was a few years older than her and lived not too far away from her as a child. She did not know what became of him in the war and assumed that he perished.

His name was everything. He was no longer a mysterious face but was becoming a person in my mind. No one on Jeanette's side of the family had heard of Horst. Mooly, whose wedding photo had led me to search for the boy's name, also reported no knowledge of his name. It seemed as if his memory on earth had disappeared with the Shoah. Could it be retrieved?

Shortly after Lilo told me Horst's name, Mooly eagerly sent me a clip of home movies that she had found among the memorabilia of Julius and Dora Klausner that she had inherited. It was a vignette of Julius and Dora at a stable they had owned or rented. (They were a wealthy couple!)

Horst Klausner, Julius Klausner, Lilo Leiser,
unknown stableboy (*left to right*) (circa 1927)

As I watched the video, I was stunned to see a scene of a young boy and a young girl coming out the stable door with Julius Klausner and a farmhand.

The boy was a perhaps twelve-year-old Horst and the girl, as Lilo soon confirmed to me by Skype as she watched the film over the internet along with me, was indeed her younger self. More than eighty years after the film had been made, Lilo and I were joyfully stunned to see a memory from her distant past come alive. The video, in which Julius and Dora are smiling and walking along with Horst and Lilo also helped me appreciate the bond that must have existed before the war between Julius and his nephew Horst. Clearly, it was strong enough that even as a child Horst would have been welcomed in his sailor suit at the white tie wedding of Horst's first cousin and Julius's daughter.

Knowing Horst's name helped me appreciate more deeply the work of Yad Vashem, the Shoah memorial center in Jerusalem, whose mission includes documenting, to the extent possible, the name and fate of every Jew who perished as a victim of the German-led onslaught on human dignity and life. Entering last name "Klausner"/first name "Horst" into the Yad Vashem website quickly brought up his final record:

Full Record Details for Klausner Horst

Source	In Memoriam - Nederlandse oorlogsslachtoffers, Nederlandse Oorlogsgravenstichting (Dutch War Victims Authority), 's-Gravenhage (courtesy of the Association of Yad Vashem Friends in Netherlands, Amsterdam)
Last Name	KLAUSNER
First Name	HORST
First Name	WILHELM
GENDER (ASSUMED)	Male
Date of Birth	27/6/1915
Place of Birth	BERLIN,BERLIN,BERLIN,GERMANY
Place of Death	SOBIBOR, Camp
Date of Death	16-7-1943
Type of material	List of victims from the Netherlands
Language	Dutch

Yad Vashem record for Horst Klausner

I now had a first name, a middle name (Wilhelm), and key biographical details. A date and place of birth (that fit with the boy in the wedding photo and with Lilo's memory) and his destiny: the death camp of Sobibór, in German-occupied Eastern Poland. The name of the death camp had achieved some publicity in popular media with its mention in the American TV mini-series *Holocaust* in 1978 and later in the 1987 British TV film *Escape from Sobibor*, documenting the October 14, 1943 uprising by the Sobibór underground. In that revolt, eleven German SS officers were killed, and about 300 prisoners escaped into the nearby forests. Most were recaptured and fewer than sixty of the escaped prisoners survived the war. The death date tells us, however, that Horst did not live long enough to participate in the famous revolt. He was one of the 200,000 people abused and murdered there. The Yad Vashem record also listed him a victim from the Netherlands, whose data had been supplied to Yad Vashem by Dutch organizations. There was now a beginning, middle, and end to his life: Berlin, the Netherlands, and Sobibór in occupied Poland.

The Holland dimension was new to me, however. Horst's spending some time there was not a total surprise, as I had already learned about German Jews from the family who had fled there as circumstances in Germany became more precarious. For most, the anticipated safety net in Holland was illusory and evaporated when the German army invaded. What had happened to Horst in the Netherlands?

With a first name and a middle name and a country to combine I could search the web for Horst Wilhelm Klausner of the Netherlands. To my delight and complete surprise not only did I find a similar (but not exact) match on a Dutch genealogy site, but I found listing of a daughter, Iris and three children belonging to her and Taco van Popta. Was this the Horst Wilhelm Klausner I was searching for, and was it possible that, somehow, he had fathered a daughter, now with three children of her own? Parsing typographic errors are part of all historical research, so while the link was not definitive, perhaps I had found a modern-day link to Horst?

Facebook gave me my answer. I couldn't find any email address or connection using Google, but Facebook, which I had joined just a few weeks before, led me to Niels van Popta, a senior executive at the internationally known Dutch brewing company Heineken. Niels accepted my "friend" request and a link was made.

Niels van Popta, Jeanette Kuvin Oren, Iris van Popta (*left to right*)
in Connecticut (2012)
ॐ

After Iris got over the surprise of newfound relatives from a distant world for her, she made plans to travel from Holland to the US. Iris naturally hoped we could provide her personal details about her father, but he was almost as new to us as to her. Nonetheless, before the year was out Iris and her son (and my new Facebook friend) Niels were visiting us in Connecticut, and we learned the rest of Horst's story. In turn, we shared the picture of the wedding photo with them and together watched the Klausner home movies showing her father (as a probable twelve- or thirteen-year-old) walking at the Klausner stable in Germany. Together with Iris and Niels we called Lilo in Argentina on Skype to introduce Lilo to her long-ago friend's daughter. And we learned how Horst's story which now lives on in Iris and her children has a beauty that balances hope against the tragedy of Horst's life.

Lilo had previously told me Horst had been the son of Julius Klausner's brother Heinrich Klausner. Horst and Heinrich are seated next to each other in the wedding photo, with Heinrich's mouth obscured by the head of Joseph Leiser.

Horst Klausner and Heinrich Klausner (mouth obscured) (May 20, 1926)

It would take me five years more after meeting Iris to put together Heinrich's genealogical record. Heinrich had also been born in Tarnów, and it was only when I was able to confirm that Heinrich Klausner had been born in 1877 as "Elchune" Klausner that I could trace his history. The Yiddish name of "Elchune" (from the Hebrew "Elchanan" meaning "God is gracious") was falsely auspicious for Heinrich's personal life. Married at age thirty-three to Else Heysemann, their daughter was born 15 months into the marriage, but lived for only a few hours. Else died just one month later. Within two years, Heinrich remarried, this time to twenty-five-year old widow Käthe (Holz) Zeimann. Within eighteen months of their marriage, Käthe gave birth to their son Horst Wilhelm on June 27, 1915. Shortly after Horst turned five, Käthe and Heinrich divorced.

Iris knew relatively little about her father Horst and his family of origin but was aware that he had left Germany in the 1930s because of the deteriorating situation for Jews there. He moved to Amsterdam, Netherlands, where he started a small textile shop, and had some connection, presumably through his uncle Julius, with the Dutch "Huff" brand shoe business. In Amsterdam, Horst rented a room in the house of a Jewish family named "de Vries." As the German menace closed around them, a romance soon blossomed between twenty-six-year-old Horst and twenty-year-old Hetty de Vries. Iris told us that Lilo's father Max Leiser had been a witness in Amsterdam to the couple's 1942 wedding, recorded in perpetuity on the marriage certificate.

In a portrait that Iris shared with us of the wedding couple, we can see the joyful light in Hetty's eyes and her cheerful gaze. The previously serious face of the young Horst is replaced by a hint of a smile in the adult. Did they have a clue on that happy day to their ill-fated future? In its own way, Horst's marriage was to be no less torn asunder than that of his parents.

Shortly after the wedding, Horst was arrested and sent to the same Westerbork transit camp where so many other Dutch Jews were housed before transfer to the death camps. His mother Käthe (who had been in forced labor since 1941) was also arrested around the same time and in 1943 deported to Auschwitz-Birkenau, never to return.[1] Hetty remained free long enough to give birth to Horst's and her daughter Iris later in 1942. Iris was told that Horst's captors gave him a surprising courtesy to see Iris shortly *after* her birth. Whether that moment of humanity amidst Horst's pathway from life to his murder actually occurred, it was erased by the subsequent German arrest of Iris's mother Hetty as well. By the time Hetty had arrived in Westerbork, Horst had already been deported to his terminal destination at Sobibór. Hetty herself was later deported from Westerbork to Auschwitz and was killed there on September 3, 1943, about six weeks after her husband Horst.

In a true act of righteousness, a newly-married young attorney and his wife Cornelisse ("Kees") Willem Dubbink and Geert Jansma Dubbink took responsibility for Horst's and Hetty's new baby Iris and sheltered her through the war, raising her as their own daughter, their only child. Postwar, the couple served as loving, foster parents.

Because of her young age, Iris could not have remembered her Horst and Hetty. She was told, however, that Horst's father—her grandfather—Heinrich Klausner had survived, gaining passage to Sao Paolo, Brazil amidst the nightmare of war.[2] Iris recalled that Horst's father Heinrich

Wedding portrait of Horst Klausner and Hettie DeVries (1942)

had some two-way correspondence with the Dubbinks after the war. At the request of the Dubbinks he sent a pair of children's shoes that were not available in the Netherlands yet at that time. Later, Heinrich may have developed some form of mental illness and the communication ended. It would be pure speculation to wonder what had befallen Heinrich. Was he experiencing an overwhelming and not uncommon and not unreasonable survivor's guilt for having survived the Shoah, after having lost his first wife to an early death, losing his second wife to an early divorce and later death in the Shoah, and finally having lost his son Horst? Did he fear that whatever home he could offer his granddaughter after the war would be inferior to the care provided by a successful attorney in postwar Holland? Was he experiencing some form of extreme mental illness that made him incapable of taking on the responsibilities of a young girl? I have not yet found the record of what became of him after his arrival in Brazil.

Strangely, although it seemed—both by virtue of Horst's appearance in the wedding photo and in the home movie with Julius and Dora Klausner—that Horst the youth (and their nephew) must have had some degree of closeness to Julius and Dora Klausner, I have not found any evidence of their having had any contact with Horst's daughter Iris after the war. It is quite likely, I believe, that they may not have even known that Horst had gotten married or even had a child. They might well have correctly assumed that Horst had been killed in the war and incorrectly assumed that he left no survivor behind. Such assumptions were not unreasonable and not uncommon in the pre-internet era. At some point postwar, Iris recently told me, there was some brief contact between her and one of Julius and Dora's daughters. But Iris was left with no sense of any close interest by that daughter in Iris. Whatever bond might have once connected Julius and Dora to Horst would not be replicated in the next generation.

The Dubbinks raised Iris in their Dutch faith as Humanists. If there are rewards in this life for the good deeds that people do, Kees and Geert Dubbink earned them and received them by protecting Iris and giving her a good home. Iris recalled that they refused any rewards later for their action, as they just "did what had to be done" in their view. During the war they also sheltered various other Jewish people in their home in Arnhem.[3] Geert lived into her nineties and Kees lived long enough to hear Iris and Niels tell their story of learning more about the origins of Iris's biological father. Kees could look back on a life of saving a child along with a distinguished legal career that led him to serve five years as President (the equivalent of Chief Justice) of the Supreme Court of the Netherlands. He died at age one hundred in 2014.

Iris grew up feeling that being a forcibly only child and the murder of her parents obligated her to bring forth a large family. She eventually married and, together with her husband, raised three children: Jelle, Nanette, and Niels. As Iris told us when we met, when she would walk down city streets with her children and grandchildren in the Netherlands, she had not forgotten her origins and would proudly say to herself, "Hitler has not won."[4]

Chapter 7

❧ THE GAON OF MARKUSZÓW ❧

$\mathscr{I}$ began this book with a story about finding my great-great grand-mother's tombstone in an abandoned and desolate cemetery in Poland. Revisiting that cemetery is where we return to come full circle.

During the 2014–2015 academic year, I had the good fortune of returning to Poland to work with my scientific colleague Professor Marek Koziorowski on our common academic pursuits. Early in my time there, I was invited to give a lecture at the thriving Kraków Jewish Community Center about my story of finding my Sarah Chana's still-standing tomb-stone some twenty years earlier. After that talk, former Oxford University social anthropologist and current professor at the Jagiellonian University in Kraków Jonathan Webber and his wife Connie invited me to their home for a meal. Over dinner and sherry, they told me about his work rebuilding a devastated Jewish cemetery in the nearby town of Brzostek, where his grandfather was born. Filmmaker Simon Target's documentary *A Town Called Brzostek* was about to be released and share this story with the world.

Beyond his scholarship Professor Webber is, if nothing else, a man of strong convictions and forceful expression. As he heard my story of finding the isolated tombstone of my ancestor still-standing in the abandoned cemetery, he demanded that I act in response. What happened in Brzostek could resonate elsewhere. Playing the vocal role of the superego, that self-critical conscience that psychoanalyst Sigmund Freud described within each of us, Professor Webber articulated what I knew inside. Fate had led my late mother and me to find a crucial and meaningful link to the past. In an abandoned cemetery that link was particularly vulnerable to permanent loss. Looking and sounding like a biblical prophet giving injunctions to his flock, Professor Webber articulated what he saw as my duty: protect the Markuszów cemetery. How to fulfill that mission was my remaining challenge.

The possibilities of accomplishing something are always greater when one can "line one's ducks in a row." In this case, the obstacles were formidable. My Polish language skills were poor. I had no local contacts in Markuszów to steer me through whatever bureaucratic requirements would need to be met. I had no idea how the local populace of Markuszów, where not a single Jew remained, would react. I knew nothing about either the religious requirements or practical aspects of rehabilitating a cemetery. I didn't have the finances to commission someone else to do the job. And this was clearly far too big a job for me to do alone. Professor Webber, however, gave me confidence that it could be done. Somehow.

A few weeks later, I spent the weekend back in my mother's hometown of Lublin. The city that had once been one-third Jewish in population and for hundreds of years a major center of Jewish self-government and Jewish scholarship, having the largest *Yeshiva* in the world before the Germans invaded, was now Jewishly a ghost of its former self. Pre-war the Jewish population had numbered 45,000. The German presence murdered at least 90 percent of those Jews and most of the survivors and their children left during the twenty-five years after the war. Today's identified Jewish population perhaps numbers fifty, including young Jews visiting from Israel for work or study. If there are more, they keep an almost invisible profile. Certainly, the great Jewish life there is gone. Aside from a few quixotic souls who were raising funds to repair an endangered wall of the one old Lublin Jewish cemetery that the Germans did not decimate, the only organized Jewish communal activity in town that I could find that year was a "pop-up" Friday night vegetarian potluck dinner and *Shabbat* service/concert organized by a budding cantor and doctoral student named Menachem Mirski.[1]

On the evening I attended, the service was attended by a diverse collection of twenty or so people of various connections to Judaism. A few were visiting Israeli students, a few were Polish Jews, a few were Poles of partial Jewish ancestry who were exploring their heritage, and a few were Poles without Jewish ancestry who were interested in exploring the Jewish side of their nation's cultural history.

Making small talk with a few of the hitherto strangers, I was delighted to meet Teresa Klimowicz, an outgoing and energetic young Polish woman. I told her about my great-great grandmother's tombstone and the abandoned cemetery in nearby Markuszów. Much to my delight, she expressed great interest and told me about her work with a Lublin-based Polish volunteer association called "*Studnia Pamięci*," the Well of Memory. The group was dedicated to studying and preserving the lost Jewish history of the Lublin area. The members had once been inspired and educated by Robert Kuwalek, a charismatic Polish Catholic histo-

Bombed synagogue of Markuszów (September 15, 1939)

rian with particular academic interest in the history of the Holocaust and the Jews of Lublin. Kuwalek had previously worked at the Majdanek (Death Camp) State Museum outside Lublin and later headed the Belzec (Death Camp) Museum. A longtime activist in building friendship between Poles and Israelis and in reclaiming and curating the lost and suppressed Jewish history of Lublin, Kuwalek was teacher and friend to the group members. His untimely and sudden death a few months before I met Teresa had left the *Studnia Pamięci* group reeling. Nonetheless, Teresa talked to me about how the association might well wish to take on Markuszów as a project. Having my personal connection to the otherwise considered anonymous past in Markuszów, she hoped, might provide the tipping point to encourage other local Poles to turn the cemetery jungle back into a cemetery. For me, the ray of hope she offered felt as welcome as manna falling from the heavens.

Jewish survivors of Markuszów bombing (September 15, 1939)

≈

Before I would leave Poland in June 2015, Teresa and her *Studnia Pamięci* colleagues Wiola Wegman and Jan Kutnik set up a meeting for us in Markuszów with Bożena Tkaczyk-Żurawska, the Secretary (Deputy Mayor) of the town and Sławomir Łowczak, the regional historian. They welcomed us warmly in the auditorium of the town hall, a building I would later learn had been built over the German-destroyed old Jewish cemetery of Markuszów, of which no trace remains. With my new Polish friends translating, Mr. Łowczak took us through the history of Markuszów and its Jewry and shared his personal collection of Markuszów photographic history. German bombings had devastated the entire town at the very start of World War II and all in town had suffered. Photos the Germans took on September 15, 1939 of the bombed-out synagogue (that had once stood next door to the current town hall) and of Jewish citizens amidst the town ruins remain poignant to this day.

Secretary Tkaczyk-Żurawska welcomed our meeting with her and offered the town's moral support. This alone was no small thing to me or to the *Studnia Pamięci* volunteers. It is one thing for an outsider to clean up a cemetery. But the effort would have no lasting effect or meaning without local support for the project. Without such support, it would be too easy for the natural law of entropy to prevail and for random vandalism or neglect to lead the cemetery back to ruin over time. And if there was opposition from the town, there would surely be bureaucratic hurdles that might prevent the work from ever being done, or worse. Fortunately, this was far from the case in Markuszów. I left the meeting with the genuine sense that Ms. Tkaczyk-Żurawska and Mr. Łowczak were equally hopeful that we could help them to reclaim their town's history and restore dignity where it had been stripped away. Ms. Tkaczyk-Żurawska told me they had hoped for this to be accomplished a few years prior when another visitor had stopped by to discuss rehabilitation of the cemetery. They reported having been supportive then, but when the visitor had looked at the actual cemetery grounds, the depth of the vegetation that had conquered the space scared him away. I left exhilarated to know that I had the support of the local Polish association and the Markuszów civic authorities.

Before departing Markuszów, Teresa, Wiola, Jan and I stopped by the Jewish cemetery to assess its status and see if we could find my great-great grandmother's tombstone that was now drawing all of us to the place. As Wiola's photo makes clear, we confirmed that cleaning the cemetery would be no simple task. I realized that I lacked the financial wherewithal to hire others to clean the cemetery, and even with the *Studnia Pamięci* volunteers, we were literally "in over our heads." But if stone can be magnetic, the psychological pull we felt from Sarah Chana's tombstone would be strong enough to help get the job done.

That cemetery in Marku-
szów is one of perhaps 1,200
abandoned and destroyed or
neglected Jewish cemeteries in
Poland under the stewardship
of a Jewish organization called
FODŻ—the Foundation for
the Preservation of Jewish
Heritage in Poland. FODŻ
was established in 2002 by the
Union of Jewish Communities
in Poland and the World Jewish Restitution Organization
(WJRO) and charged with the
gargantuan task of protecting
and managing the abandoned
cemeteries and synagogues
that are the authentic physical

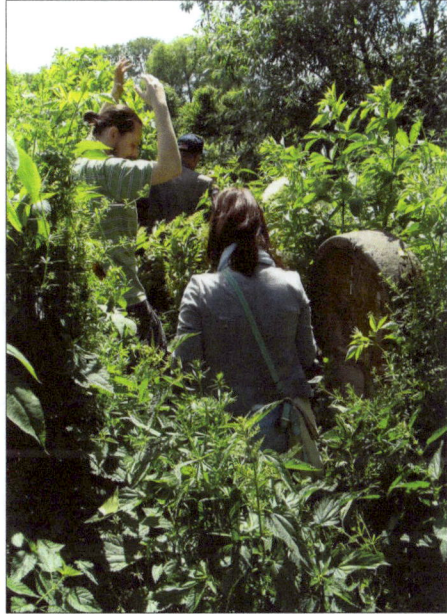

Jan Kutnik, Dan Oren,
Teresa Klimowitz (*left to right*)
in Markuszów Jewish Cemetery
(June 26, 2015)
❧

memory of some 900 years of Jewish life in Poland. With a small budget
sourced from German and other European restitution funds and occasional donations from Jewish supporters around the world, FODŻ does
all it can to save and preserve the sites it can protect, but the magnitude
of the task is overwhelming compared to the resources available.[2]

Aristotle is credited with having said that "nature abhors a vacuum."
In Markuszów and other Jewish cemeteries the void has sometimes been
filled with dense vegetation and sometimes trash. But the void of human
decency in Polish Jewish cemeteries is being filled by an amazing Christian group I was introduced to by FODŻ called "The *Matzevah* Foundation."[3] Over a Skype phone call to Poland, I learned from minister-leader

Steven Reece about his group's devoted work. For several summers, Steven and his flock (mostly Baptists from the US south) had been travelling to Poland as volunteers to do the physical labor of caring for and restoring Jewish cemeteries. In their use of an ancient Hebrew phrase, the *Matzevah* group seeks to do *"tikkun olam"*—repairing the world. For them, as a fulfillment of their personal obligation to make the world a better place, they have chosen—as devout Christians—to work to bring about reconciliation and heal the pain caused to Jews by Christians—as they frame it—during the years of the Shoah. While no one has the power to raise the dead or erase the past, they are determined to do what they can to improve the future. And they do so through the cemetery work in summer, and then by educating people about the Shoah year-round.

Steven was particularly intrigued as his group had never worked in partnership with Jews from outside of Poland. And it was not for lack of his trying to engage Jews, particularly American and Israeli Jews, in partnership. Steven had encountered at least three obstacles in trying to recruit American Jewish support. Foremost, for many Jews of Polish descent, the horrors of the Shoah experienced by the Jews of Poland had firmly shut their minds to any desire to have anything ever again to do with Poland—even if that experience was driven by Nazi Germany. It was a terrible traumatic chapter from their personal, family, or communal histories that they wished to keep sealed. Secondly, for others, Poland's mixed record regarding Jews before and after the Shoah made it harder for Steven to find American Jewish allies. On one hand, pre-Second World War Poland had been one of the more tolerant countries in the world toward Jews for centuries. On the other hand, bigotry and violence was sometimes real. During the war there were undoubtedly examples of Poles who passively or actively collaborated with Germans in the murder of Jews. As many know in the case of the intra-war massacre of Jews by

Polish Christians in Jedwabne, Poland, it has not been easy for many Poles to acknowledge this failure in their communal moral compass by some of their members.[4] To add insult to injury, many of the few Polish Jewish survivors of the Shoah tried to return to their homes and found that other Poles had occupied them and were not about to yield them to their rightful owners. To the date of this writing, the vast majority of Jewishly-owned private property that was taken in the 1940s in Poland has not been not restored to the rightful owners or heirs. An infamous *pogrom* led by Polish soldiers, police, and civilians in Kielce in July 1946 killed forty-two Jews and wounded dozens of others. Such violence could not be blamed on Germany or Nazis, but rather stained the country's record. Fearing for their lives, unable to reclaim their homes, tens of thousands of Jews fled Poland in the aftermath. A 1968 Polish anti-Zionism campaign led most of the remaining 30,000 Jews in Poland (1 percent of the number there before the Shoah) to flee the country. Finally, for yet other Jews, learning about this American Christian group seeking to work in Jewish cemeteries in Poland, there was some uncertainty about what the *Matzevah* Foundation's motives were. Were they seeking Jewish money to further their private interests? Were they seeking to convert the Jews with whom they hoped to work? Why would they be such "do-gooders"?

As Steven and I spoke over the course of a few Skype calls, I became convinced of his integrity and of his genuine selflessness and that of his group, whom I would later come to imagine almost as a flock of human angels on earth. Steven invited me to come work with his group a few weeks after my call in the Polish town of Oświęcim where they were scheduled to be working again for a week in the Jewish cemetery there. The city had achieved world infamy because of the German construction of the nearby death camps known as Auschwitz I and Auschwitz II-Birkenau. I took a discount Wizz Air flight to Poland, where Steven picked me up. There I spent two days working with the group of Christian volunteers and a group of European twenty-somethings who had joined them to study at the International Youth Meeting Center in Oświęcim at night and to clean the devastated Oświęcim Jewish cemetery during the day. In the oppressive heat they worked through and in a cooler evening, I got to know Steven and some of his group and share with them in the extraordinary work of their lives. Among these remarkable souls, for example, was Nashville Christian book store buyer Rachel McRae, who carried her youthful charm and energy wherever she went. Young Polish man Przemysław Panasiuk never showed a moment of tiredness nor let discouragement cloud his good humor. As dedicated as each of these Christians were to their religious tradition, I was touched by their genuine inquisitiveness about Judaism.

There is a famous Talmudic saying that the world stands on three pillars. In liberal translation, one could say they are: the study of Scripture, prayer to God, and acts of human kindness.[5] Spending two days with the *Matzevah* Foundation group in Oświęcim, sweeping, weeding, lopping tree limbs, and moving heavy tombstones or their fragments, I saw them do it all. Without exaggeration, they were the kind of incredible souls whose presence you spend time with and walk away from afterwards feeling unworthy to share the same earth with. They were fun to be with and over-the-top funny! They made no effort to convert anybody. Rather they wanted to create dialogue, connect people, and build hope. And they had the potential to help me with my cemetery in Markuszów. Of course, they were interviewing me as well to see if my project was a good match for them. With so many abandoned Jewish cemeteries in Poland and their volunteer and financial capacity limited to working on just a handful each summer, their potential workload was enough to keep their group busy for centuries. Their work in restoring a dignified resting place to anonymous thousands carried no reward. And, as Jewish burial societies note, the caring for the remains of the dead is a kind of task where the true beneficiary can never repay the kindness. Yet, for the *Matzevah* Foundation group, they concluded that the potential of restoring a cemetery where an ancestor of a working volunteer was part of the effort might be an added bonus, providing an additional level of meaning.

Two months later, at their annual board meeting in Nashville, Tennessee, The *Matzevah* Foundation group decided to partner with me and the Poles of *Studnia Pamięci* to clean the Jewish cemetery of Markuszów, under the auspices of FODŻ.

In return, my wife Jeanette and I recruited a group of eleven friends and family to work in partnership: our daughters and son-in-law were lovingly persuaded into joining the expedition with six dear friends from our home area of New Haven, Connecticut who volunteered for a Summer 2016 journey to Poland. Though the group was large, our expenses were within reason, as the US dollar was strong relative to the Polish złoty and we stayed in rustic, almost communal, "agrotourism" housing while working at the cemetery.

When we arrived in Poland our friends and family group took a few days to see some of Poland's tourist sites, including the amazing POLIN museum of Polish Jewish history in Warsaw and the beauty of Kraków. We enjoyed a Shabbat dinner amidst the vitality of the Jewish Community Center of Kraków.

On the way to Kraków, we detoured to Tarnów, the Polish city where Jeanette's Ettinger, Leiser, and Taubenschlag ancestors had all lived for much of the nineteenth century and prior. In Tarnów we had the privilege of being taken to the Jewish cemetery by Adam Bartosz, a historian who is the world's authority on the history of the decimated Jewish and Gypsy communities there. Over decades, seemingly singlehandedly, he built up and directed the Tarnów Regional Museum and founded the Tarnów Committee for the Protection of Monuments of Jewish Culture. Bartosz has directed the restoration of the Tarnów Jewish cemetery site of thousands of destroyed, damaged, and neglected tombstones.[6]

Our jam-packed schedule just allowed us a short time to wander through the cemetery looking for relatives. I reminded Jeanette that the family surnames we were hunting for in Tarnów were Ettinger, Leiser, and Taubenschlag. From a distance, Jeanette looked over to me and said that discovering one would be like finding a "needle in a haystack." I switched metaphors and called back to her, "no, it would be like being struck by lightning." And then the figurative lightning struck. As I was looking due east, about thirty feet away from me, I saw a piece of a tombstone fallen on the ground sitting slightly upward at just the perfect angle so that from a distance I could clearly read the Germanic surname on the stone: Taubenschlag. I called out to Jeanette and then to my daughters Sarah and Amalyah and then to the rest of our group, as we saw the base of what had once been the tombstone of Josef Taubenschlag, deceased September 29, 1912.

I then recognized another piece of toppled granite nearby that looked as if it would have fit perfectly on the base of Josef's stone. Except for its fallen state, the blank column-like top looked in near perfect condition. Adam Bartosz came over and, based on his extensive understanding of the tombstones of that cemetery, confidently stated that we would find Hebrew writing on the side of the tombstone that lay facing the ground, likely in that position for at least the prior seventy or more years. The hefty weight of the granite pieces had surely protected them since they had been toppled. It took the combined strength of one cemetery worker and all the men in our group (especially that of my son-in-law Mike) and a shovel used as a lever to tip the column to be

ABOVE: Amalyah and Jeanette Kuvin Oren (*left to right*) and part of
Josef Taubenschlag's tombstone, Tarnów Jewish cemetery (2016)

BELOW: Pieces of Josef Taubenschlag's tombstone (2016)

visible face-up. Lo and behold, Adam was right. A Hebrew epitaph told us this was the grave marker of Rabbi Josef Taubenschlag, with critical additional information in the Hebrew that he was the son of Rafael Taubenschlag.

The given name of "Josef" was unknown to me among Jeanette's Taubenschlags, but the name Rafael was not. Jeanette's great-great-great-great grandfather had been Rafael Taubenschlag of Tarnów. Was this perhaps a son of his? That evening I connected to the internet and the Jewish Records Indexing-Poland database of Tarnów that had been organized by volunteer Howard Fink. With the assistance of a table Howard had prepared for me well before, and the guidance of "Jewish Tarnow" Facebook group expert Russ Maurer, I quickly found the online death record of Josef, son of Rafael and Zysl.

In that moment, genealogy came alive. My wife and I were able to introduce our daughters to the tombstone of their hitherto unknown (to them and to any other known living relative) great-great-great-great-great uncle. An extremely distant relation to be sure, yet a tangible connection to the past. I have not yet been able to find whether any direct descendants of Josef are alive today. (At least one adult child of his was killed in the Shoah.) With the contributions from ten of the Taubenschlag cousins from around the world that I could track down, Rabbi

Death record of Josef Taubenschlag (1912)

Taubenschlag's grave was rebuilt with Adam Bartosz's help, and that tombstone again stands tall honoring his life of good work.

Two days after our trip to Tarnów, our group proceeded to my mother's hometown of Lublin. There we met Steven Reece and the *Matzevah* Foundation team and Teresa Klimowicz and her *Studnia Pamięci* colleagues. Teresa led all of us on the wrenching walking tour of the grounds of the Majdanek death camp adjacent

Restored tombstone of Josef Taubenschlag (2016)

to the city of Lublin. For my group of friends and family, it was difficult enough to see the tombstone fragments that had been made into street pavement, the endless field where a few barracks still stood, the trenches where victims were shot, the gas chambers where victims were poisoned, the crematorium where bodies were incinerated, and the still-present pile of ashes. If there was an ounce of consolation on the visit, it was having non-Jews with us. The unforgivable guilt for the crimes of the Shoah was not a guilt that they bore either by their personal behavior or that of their ancestors. Yet something was calling to each one of them to try and bring healing to the abominable crime whose most prominent emblems today are the death camps such as Majdanek. And these American Baptists and non-Jewish Poles were willing to give their time, money, and sweat to help bring healing. Such good actions are too rare in a world driven by self-interest, and I remain grateful.

That evening my friends and family and the Matzevah Foundation volunteers settled into the agrotourism hotel just outside the town of

Markuszów where my great-great grandmother's cemetery was located. Eager to find a place of lodging where we could live communally and inexpensively for the four workdays ahead, we hoped the hotel would live up to its advertising. The photo on the website portrayed a large, beautiful building that looked like it could accommodate our group. When we arrived, we discovered that the photo on the website was not actually our hotel, but rather a local tourist attraction. While nineteen lodgers sharing three toilets and three showers (with enough hot water to allow three people to have a hot shower per day) indeed provided cramped living conditions, they provided memories that all of us can laugh at to this day. Co-owner Barbara Pawłowska and her family went out of their way to attend to the first Americans they had ever hosted, and the largest group of guests that had ever stayed at their hotel. For our group of Jewish lodgers, most of whom would not eat meat products that were not kosher, Barbara—with characteristic Polish hospitality towards guests—prepared tasty vegetarian meals for us for the four days. I was touched that the Christians, who had no food restrictions to limit them, chose to eat vegetarian themselves for the four and one-half days with us. For them it was both a way of demonstrating solidarity with us and, on a practical level, simplifying the work of Barbara and her staff in preparing our meals. Such demonstrations of affinity did not go unnoticed.

The work at the cemetery itself was hard yet rewarding. When we arrived we found the untamed jungle we had been expecting. We would benefit over the four work days from beautiful weather. Each day was sunny and dry, with warm, but not oppressive, temperatures. Using bushwhacking tools, saws, rakes, shovels, and brushes brought by the Christian volunteers and grit that we each displayed, we cleaned virtually every corner of the American football field-sized ground. Beyond vege-

Markuszów Jewish Cemetery (2016)
ஐ

tation, in one corner we found years of rubbish likely deposited by young people using the cemetery as a place to hide and get drunk and in another corner years of chaff likely deposited as agricultural debris. The decades old trees that had been planted after World War II were left untouched, but the trash and the 1.4 acres of wild bush that covered the grounds was gradually cut away.

As we chopped, cut, and dragged brush and tree limbs, local neighbors stopped by to see what we were doing. One man told us about his mother, whom he said had hidden a Jewish family during the war in her home in today's Ukraine. Another told of hearing reports from his father of Jews from the area on two occasions having been brought to the cemetery by German soldiers and then murdered in mass executions. He showed us the two depressions in the cemetery grounds that were the spots of those killings. He recalled being told that after the executions, local Christian Poles were paid by the Germans to bury the newly-shot Jews. Earth that we had been walking over repeatedly suddenly evoked awe.

Town secretary Bożena (who had arranged to clear the grown-over branches that had previously blocked the driveway into the cemetery) brought Mayor Andrzej Rozwałka to share in the hope engendered by the cleaning of the burial grounds and to cheer us on. She then escorted me and one of the Polish group on a door-to-door walk around the neighborhood of the cemetery in knocking-on-house-doors political diplomacy. Inviting each of the residents at home to come to the rededication ceremony we would have later in the week, Bożena (we were now on a first-name basis) would assure the neighbors that our cleaning presence was endorsed by the town and try to make a personal connection between me (a "descendant of Markuszów") and the locals. Bożena also connected me back to Paweł Sygowski, the historian I mentioned back in chapter One who had first found the documents that helped me prove my great-grandfather Icek Erych Rozenberg was, in fact, the son of Sarah Chana, whose tombstone had ignited the genealogical quest that had brought Jews and Christians, Americans and Poles (and even a German) to clean up Sarah Chana's final resting place. I had not previously realized that Paweł had his own personal connection to this very cemetery. In 1992, one year before my mother and I had first visited the Markuszów Jewish cemetery together, Paweł had begun a mapping and documentation project at that same cemetery. Paweł had once shown Bożena his "treasure map" of the surviving tombstones at the cemetery. She invited him to come join our group of rescuers.

I knew where in the cemetery Sarah Chana's grave was; discovering further artifacts was like a scavenger hunt. Once Paweł arrived on our

Paweł Sygowski, Caylee Dugger, Jan Kutnik, Rachel McRae,
Regina Menke (*left to right*) at Markuszów Jewish Cemetery (2016)

second day, we would no longer be operating blindly. Paweł quickly took a vine-cutter and joined us in the tedious work of removing foliage. By the end of the day's work we had cleared out enough of the foliage to reach Sarah Chana's tombstone. Everyone stopped the work to come see the lodestone of our mission to Markuszów. One hundred and fourteen years after Sarah Chana's remains had been placed in the ground, her tombstone—still in its original place had survived and brought awe and satisfaction to every member of our group. With the tombstone in site, Paweł pulled out his meticulous map and showed us that entirely unanticipated treasures were in store. At map top were two circles indicating the sites of the mass graves. Detailed throughout were the sites of the surviving individual tombstones or fragments. Most of them were still hidden under a layer of dirt that Paweł had used to protect them from the elements and vandalism after his 1992 survey was completed. Paweł also pulled out a

Tombstone album of
Paweł Sygowski (2016)

photo album that he had assembled decades before with photos linked to
the map locations and identifying information (to the extent he had it) for
those named on the tombstones. We were stunned. We had arrived at the
cemetery thinking that we might find the ten or so remaining tombstones
that I had previously encountered on a walk around the cemetery, most
of which are documented in an online database. Pawel's records showed
there were at least ten times that number still surviving the devastation.

My own favorite was the intricately carved headstone of a certain
Moshe Aryeh. With the stone lying face back on the ground after we
had uncovered it, its artwork was exquisite. A near-perfect and life-like
stone arm and hand, presumably that of Moshe Aryeh, seemed almost
to be reaching out from the grave to pull out a carved book (perhaps the
biblical Book of Exodus) from a carved cabinet. It was a stunning testimony both to the deceased's love of Torah learning and the skill of the
anonymous stonecutter.

Paweł's greatest gift was the unanticipated one he offered after
we had sawed, cut, and cleared our way to my great-great-grandmother
Sarah Chana's tombstone. "You know," he told us, "I think that her father
is buried in the row just one row away." This was a total surprise to me.
I was well aware, by then, that Sarah Chana's father had been Chaim

Tombstone of Moshe Aryeh (2016)

Jankiel Kohen, one-time chief rabbi of Markuszów. Over the years I had imagined clearing our way to Sarah Chana's tombstone. I had never even considered the possibility that we might also find that of her father. Consulting his map and album, Paweł led us about twenty feet away from Sarah Chana's burial space. I learned then that in this cemetery, not unlike others belonging to religious Jewish communities in that era, men were buried in rows separate from women. Paweł gently tested the site where his map indicated Chaim Jankiel's grave might be found. Quickly enough he found the spot and we started brushing away the dirt covering his tombstone. We uncovered the broken headstone presumably knocked to the ground about seven decades before. It was a double stone and a double-find for us! On the left was a clear inscription for Yehuda Aryeh Rozenberg, Sarah Chana's husband, my great-great grandfather!

Joint tombstone of Yehuda Aryeh Rozenberg and
Rabbi Chaim Yankel Kohen (2016)

On the right side of the stone was an inscription for his father-in-law, Sarah Chana's father, my great-great-great grandfather, Rabbi Chaim Jankiel Kohen, chief rabbi of the community. The very middle word in the very middle line of his epitaph read "הגאון," the "Gaon," echoing to the modern ear the title given to the famous eighteenth century Talmud scholar Rabbi Eliyahu ben Shlomo Zalman, the famous "Gaon of Vilna." As I likely share only about 3 percent of my DNA with Rabbi Kohen, I can't claim any dramatic biological structure from him, but I couldn't minimize the wonder I felt being in the surprisingly tangible presence of an ancestor who had died in 1885, was later virtually erased from history by the Shoah, and was somehow being brought back to consciousness 131 years later. So much of Jewish life in Poland had been destroyed by the Second World War and its aftermath. Yet, just a few inches below the surface, powerful connections remained.

On the last of our four days of hard work, with the former jungle having been fully cleared and now visibly a cemetery once again, our group conducted a rededication ceremony. It had not been my idea to have one and I had not initially seen a need for one. I had organized the group effort, not for pomp and circumstance and not for publicity, but for the sake of the work itself. It was to protect the memory of those who were buried behind the one surviving wall and three vanished walls of the cemetery boundary. I will always be grateful that Steven Reece of The Matzevah Foundation convinced me I was wrong. Always respectful of Jewish customs, of the holiness of a burial ground, and of the awkwardness of Christians and Jews together on the blood-stained soil of Poland, Steven urged us to organize a dedication ceremony. A veteran of multiple cemetery clean-ups, Steven knew from experience the value to those who had done the work, and equally importantly, the value to the local Polish community of formal acknowledgment of the work that had been done.

The dead can never thank cemetery volunteers for their work; it takes a ceremony to give that work meaning.

On Thursday afternoon, scores of local townspeople gathered at the chairs that the town had set up at the entrance to the cemetery area. The people who had visited us during the week returned with friends and neighbors. The farmer next door, who had previously lamented to us regarding the disrepair of the cemetery, joined the solemn exercise. Another descendant of Chana Sarah, Moshe Zukerman, a cousin of my mother's whose side of the family had been estranged from my mother's side for almost fifty years, flew in from China along with his wife for the event. The distance of time and deeds of goodwill could heal alienations from the past. Indeed, that was an underlying theme of the day.

Regina Menke, a young German woman volunteering in the clean-up with the Polish *Studnia Pamięci* group, took out her violin and opened the ceremony by playing the haunting music of *Prayer from "Jewish Life"* #1 by Ernest Bloch. Speeches in Polish by Mayor Rozwałka and regional historian Łowczak recognized the town's Jewish history and welcomed the presence of Jews in Markuszów that week. Representatives from the US embassy and the Poland Chief rabbi's office lent civil and Jewish religious authority to the proceedings. I had asked my young adult daughters Sarah (pregnant with our future first grandchild) and Amalyah to share with Steven Reece the honor of placing small stones of memory upon the large marker that had been erected at the entrance to the cemetery, now unmistakably marking it in Polish and English as a cherished site. As a parent, I was naturally proud to be able to see my daughters in this special role. As an American Jew, I had been living in what then seemed like the halcyon times of 2016 when Jews felt so comfortable in America that it was easy to forget one's heritage. On this occasion, I was overwhelmed with joy to see my daughters palpably enter

Amalyah Oren, Sarah Oren Brasky, Reverend Steven Reece (*left to right*)
at dedication of memorial marker at Markuszów Jewish cemetery (July 21, 2016)

into a world of their ancestors for a brief moment that I think will be part of their permanent memory. On other occasions, their eyes might glaze over if I talked history to them. On this day, their eyes filled with tears when they could feel the beauty of that history in the midst of a no-longer-abandoned cemetery. Through the illustrations on the tombstones and the names, dates and words of love inscribed on them, the beauty of a lost world was still very much alive.

Steven's Matzevah Foundation had organized and led all of our work efforts and had paid for half of that memorial stone out of their boundless generosity. All week he and his colleagues had spoken of their gratitude to me and my family and friends for the service they were able to perform to restore dignity to the burial grounds of our ancestors. For every word they spoke, their actions resonated one hundred-fold.

Markuszow Jewish cemetery clean-up crew (July 20, 2016)

Five days of touring, dining, laughing, working, singing and even a few moments of study and ecumenical prayer together had transcended gene-alogy, history and religion, having simply become life. When our work group posed together with Mayor Rozwałka in front of the cemetery marker, the smiles on our faces bore permanent witness to the friends we had become. Decades of neglect had been replaced with a summer of hope. Of course, vegetation would overtake the cemetery again, but with annual, inexpensive cleanings, the flora could be kept in check.

Perhaps the most powerful words of the ceremony were delivered by Mieczysław Cisło, Auxiliary Bishop of the Archdiocese of Lublin, Vicar General of the Archdiocese of Lublin, and Chairman of the Board and Religious Dialogue Committee Chairman for Dialogue with Jews for the

Bishop Mieczysław Cisło speaking at Markuszów Jewish
cemetery dedication ceremony (July 21, 2016)
ॐ

Polish Bishop's Conference. Jew, Catholic, Protestant, atheist, American
and Pole were all touched and surely many were surprised. Just his attendance was extraordinary. Such a high-ranking bishop had never visited
the small town before. His very presence made it clear to all this was
no ordinary day. His regal bearing conveyed his authority. In the formal
speech (given in Polish and translated into English) and in numerous
personal interactions, Bishop Cisło humbly guided his Catholic flock
to love those of their "older brother" faith of Judaism and to honor the
newly-cleaned, sacred Jewish cemetery grounds in Markuszów. He told
the townspeople it was their duty to protect this sacred ground in their
own town. He talked about the loss that Poland suffers to this day in no
longer having a Jewish community. He spoke of the valuable meaning

of a permanent home for Jews in Israel. He expressed the hope that one day Lublin's *Yeshivat Chokhmei Lublin*—once the largest *Yeshiva* in the world, today a hotel—would again host young rabbinical students. I was not the only one there to feel tears coming to the eyes as I listened to his beacon of hope and positivity. And then, with the ceremony over, and the bishop having no more ceremonial obligations or social pleasantries required, the bishop's generous spirit surfaced yet again. One of the town officials had told the bishop about the discovery of the grave and marker of my great-great-great grandfather, Rabbi Chaim Kohen, the "Gaon of Markuszów." His duties complete, the bishop could have walked back to his car and returned to the Archdiocese in Lublin. Instead, Bishop Cisło walked out to the cemetery wall, at the southeast of the cemetery, in the corner closest to Jerusalem where Rabbi Kohen was buried and chose to pay his respects to the long-deceased religious head of the Markuszów Jewish community. A humble man-of-faith honored the memory of a fellow man-of-faith.

There is a Talmudic fantasy that if every Jew in the world were just to keep one Sabbath, then the messiah would come soon. I could not help but think that if every Christian and every Jew in the world were just to hear the message of hope that Bishop Cisło was preaching, or just to spend a few days working with Steven Reece and his Matzevah Foundation volunteers, or work alongside Paweł Sygowski and Teresa Klimowicz and the Studnia Pamięci group, the messiah would surely come soon as well.

Chapter 8

—❖ FINAL RESTING PLACE ❖—

*E*arlier, I shared the apocryphal and humorous family story of Philip Roth greeting a relative who had found her way to his doorstep in her genealogical pursuit of family. Excited to meet the renowned author, she introduced herself, described their familial connection, to which he replied, "So, what?"

"So, what?" is the question that I've had to ask myself along the way. Is the world a better place if we pursue genealogy? Would my time have been better spent or enjoyed serving food to the poor in a soup kitchen, helping indigent patients in a mental health clinic, getting active in a political campaign, or going to a football game played by my beloved Green Bay Packers? Fortunately, for me, as for most of us in the developed world, there is time enough in life for all such activities of giving, of advocacy, and of pleasure, alongside the task of earning our daily bread.

Having grown up in a home and educational system from grade school through university that respected and encouraged the pursuit and dissemination of knowledge, sharing what I learned of the family stories along the way with other family was a natural process. If fellow family members are not interested in their background, why should outsiders care? Not every family member, of course, finds such stories meaningful. As I thought that some of the stories I learned along the way *were* truly interesting, I shared them with those who would listen, and I've collected them in this book. There are stories of distant family members I haven't repeated. In one case, sharing the details of the murder-suicide I learned concerning a father distraught about his son's intractable illness serves no use besides to amplify whatever residual pain must exist in those closest to those long-gone family members. In another case I discovered a scoundrel who filed a false claim that resulted in the improper diversion of a portion of another branch of that family's inheritance. By the time the victim learned of the incident (years after it had occurred, and surely beyond the statute of limitations), the offender was quite elderly and the victim chose not to pursue the matter. Nonetheless, I did not want to give the "false filer" one mention by name, lest his unethical behavior be honored by the recollection of his name.

This book is certainly not intended as a way to brag about the names or actions of illustrious ancestors or cousins one never knew about whom one has encountered in this quest for family history. As a non-Jewish friend recently emphasized to me about his own distinguished ancestor dating to the time of the founding of the United States, his upbringing strictly looked down on the idea of claiming fame based on a relative. In the end, no matter how meritorious or despicable an ancestor might be, we are all judged on the basis of our own actions. While our relatives' résumé might help some get admitted to Stanford or Harvard or Princeton or Yale, those relatives do not make us better or worse persons. Indeed, even if one of us does have a major or minor celebrity (as opposed to a rogue) as an ancestor or third cousin twice-removed, surely most of our family immediate and extended, and most likely ourselves, are quite ordinary people. Jewish oral law explains that humankind was first created in the singular form of Adam so that no one would claim, "My ancestors are better than yours."[1] A host of websites such as Ancestry.com, Geni.com, MyHeritage.com, not to mention the DNA testing companies, are proliferating and linking each of us to each other in previously unimaginable ways, supporting the notion that we are all somehow cousins. And lest we become too impressed with our ancestors, the reality of life is that we all end up as dust in the ground.

So why pursue genealogy? How do we answer Philip Roth if he asks, "So, what"? (And, in fairness to him, when my wife and his second cousin once-removed Jeanette asked him a genealogical question, he couldn't have been more kind in his response.) My brief answers to the "So what" question for each of us are the kinds of stories this book finds. The uninitiated might think that genealogy is an incredibly dull and dusty enterprise—pursued in dim archives and spent compiling boring lists of names, dates, and locations. And if you think that, you are missing the forest for the trees. Because I can promise you that if you pursue *your* own history you will discover many of the most fascinating stories on earth, that are *your* family's history. This pursuit will take you to corners of the world you never imagined and to meet the most interesting of people, alive and dead! Names, dates, and locations are a doorway to the past, a seemingly boring, dusty, doorway. But when you pursue those details, you will find that doorway opening a world of the most interesting of stories. In every culture, stories are the true currency of a rich life. As a beloved psychiatry professor once taught me, "Everyone has a story." And so many of those tales—especially about those for whom evil snuffed out their memory—are worth telling and retelling. Pursuing those stories will make your life and the lives of those you love all the richer. Not in terms of finances, but in meaning. We may never know "why" any of us are on this earth, but finding meaning yields a priceless inheritance to pass on to future generations.

Anthropologist Kaja Finkler, on reading this manuscript, reminds me that the lens of genealogy provides a framework for understanding our personal past and addressing some of the mysteries of individuals otherwise lost to history.[2] Genealogy can lead to solving those mysteries and giving voice to individuals and communities that would otherwise be lost to memory or relegated to antiquarian charts. Genealogical history gives temporality and continuity to our lives, and meaning regarding where we came from, particularly as we live in a modern age when most people grow up knowing only the present. A genealogy gives us an insight into who we are and where we came from, basic existential questions ignored in the busyness and homogeneity of modern life.

What spurred me initially to go on my genealogical quest was the realization that I knew more about the Derby, Connecticut Pinto family genealogy and history than I knew about my own. Perhaps, you, dear reader, might by now be saying you know more about the Oren family history than you do about your own. If so, then now is the time to begin changing that. Good luck!

Appendix 1

THE WEDDING PHOTO
(*Additional People*)

The numbers in parentheses after people's names refer to their location in the wedding photo in Chapter Five.

JACOB ROSNER (2): Jacob (Jak) immigrated to Palestine in 1936, where he worked as a photographer for the Jewish National Fund. He died in Tel Aviv at age forty-seven in 1950.

OSCAR (6), SIDONIE (SARAH ZALDE) (7), AND ELSA ROSNER (17): Not surprisingly, father-of-the-groom Oscar was also in the shoe business and owned a shoe factory. Mooly introduced me by e-mail to Oscar and Sidonie's granddaughter (daughter of Jacob from his second marriage) Noemi Schwarz and Noemi told me and Mooly the identities of these three in the photo. Noemi reported that Oscar died of natural causes before the war, but Sidonie and their daughter (Jacob's sister) Elsa perished during the war. Already living in Palestine before the war, Jacob was able to get the British Mandate authorities to issue a permit for his sister Elsa to move from Germany to Palestine. But, as Noemi reported, when Elsa was about to leave Germany, she decided that she could not leave her mother behind and she decided to return to her mother's side. In the end, Sidonie was arrested and then three days later her daughter Elsa was arrested as well. Both perished at Auschwitz-Birkenau death camp.

ILSE KLAUSNER (10) AND KÄTHE KLAUSNER: Ilse and Käthe were bride Margot's (1) two sisters. Following a failed first marriage, Ilse married philosopher Arnold Metzger. Hoping to escape the Germans their family immigrated to France in 1938. When Germany invaded France in 1940, Metzger gathered the family's jewelry and traded it for a fisherman's boat ride to Jersey, a British island between France and England. They boarded a freighter there and made their way to Britain, where Ilse and Arnold were briefly imprisoned as suspected Nazi infiltrators. Ilse's three children were placed in an orphanage, where they were kept safe and well-treated. Ilse's parents Julius and Dora were able to arrange for Ilse's family to travel to the US via Argentina, which they did in 1941 prior to the US entry to the war. In the US the family settled in Cambridge, Massachusetts for Arnold to teach at Simmons College, and for all of them to bask in the aura of Harvard University. Ilse eventually returned to her native Germany, worked as an editor and died in Munich in 1980. Her son Thomas Albert Metzger became a professor specializing in Chinese intellectual and institutional history. This summary history was shared with me by Thomas's daughter Julie Kornack.

Ilse's sister Käthe does not appear in the photo, but I am convinced
she was also present at the wedding, as the program (provided by Mooly)
for the humorous *spiel* (performance) put on at the wedding lists Käthe
as a dancer under her (briefly) married name of Käthe Neumann. I speculate that a few of the attendees at the wedding may not have been in
the photo as they may have been dressing for a humorous post-wedding
play that they were about to perform in honor of the bride and groom.
(The *spiel* program is titled "Jak und Margot: Allegorisches Drama in
fünf Akten.") Käthe lived much of her post-war life as a single woman in
Vienna, where she died at the age 107 in 2009. The wedding photo from
Käthe's drawer is the primary source for chapter five.

FRIEDERIKE (FANNY) (NÉE KLAUSNER) HULLES (3) AND MEYER HULLES
(4): Julius' sister Fanny moved to Meyer's residence of Vienna where they
were married in 1891. Meyer died two years after this photo was taken.
Fanny and her son Emil ran the Austrian "Hermes" shoe company and
she owned a small stake in the larger Del-Ka shoe company led by her
brother Ludwig Klausner in Vienna. She and Emil were both arrested
after the Anschluss, Emil being sent to Dachau and Buchenwald, much
like his uncle Ludwig Klausner. Despite the arrests, Fanny and Meyer
and Emil's brother Paul and Paul's wife were all able to gain passage from
Holland to safety in the US in 1938 and 1939. Hermes was confiscated
from them entirely.

GISELA (NÉE ETTINGER) LEISER (9) AND BENNO LICHTMANN (31): Gisela's first husband, egg-dealer turned shoe magnate Hermann Leiser died
young at age fifty-one in 1910. Gisela later married Benno Lichtmann,
who died four years after the photo was taken at age sixty-four. I have
not learned Gisela's exact timeline nor route of passage out of Germany,

but Lilo recalled that Gisela was able to travel to Palestine (where her granddaughter Margot then lived) during the war years and then in 1949 Gisela moved to Argentina to live with her daughter Dora and son-in-law Julius Klausner. Gisela died in Buenos Aires in 1952 at age eighty-seven. My wife Jeanette is a great-great-granddaughter of Gisela.

JOHANNA (24) AND SALOMON ETTINGER (33), ALICE ETTINGER (50), GERHARD (76) AND PAULA ROEMER (75): Lilo's study of the wedding photo led her to identify her great uncle Salomon Ettinger. Some further research led me to the exciting news that Salomon's grandson and Lilo's second cousin Michael Roemer had also been teaching at nearby Yale for more than forty years. Learning his story was simply a matter of Jeanette and I inviting him over for coffee. It felt almost surreal for Jeanette to discover a second cousin of her grandmother spending half the year teaching just a few miles from us! Not only that, but a noted film-maker who directed what may have been the first feature film produced by a college student, and later wrote and directed the critically-acclaimed film *Nothing But a Man*, considered one of the best films ever made in the US about the life of African-Americans. Michael later recalled that his family's experience as Jews in Germany helped sensitize him to understand more about the life of African-Americans in the US.

At our home, we were delighted to chat extensively with this cheerful man whose Berlin accent reminded us of Jeanette's late grandmother Edith. Roemer studied the wedding photo he had never previously seen that had been taken two years before his birth. He quickly recognized his Ettinger grandparents, his parents, and his aunt. His grandfather Salomon was an uncle of Jeanette's great-grandmother Fella, whose lineage began this chapter. Born in the Austrian Empire town of Tarnów, Galicia (today's Poland), Salomon was also a shoemaker and made the first of many trips to the US as an approximately fifteen-year-old in the mid-1880s along with his older brother Arnold to live and work in Bamberg, South Carolina. That young age allowed him to learn to speak English with an American—and not a German—accent. He later returned to Berlin, where the Klausner family shoe business was growing, in order to marry Johanna. In Berlin he owned—apparently in partnership with his niece's husband Max Pollak (11)—Ettingers Schuhwarenhaus, as depicted in a postage stamp advertisement from about 1910.

Salomon's sisters Gisele (also an Ettinger, and Jeanette's great-great grandmother) and Marie were grandmothers of the bride, so with a double personal family connection and surely an intimate shoe business connection, Salomon and Johanna's presence (and that of their two daughters and son-in-law) at the wedding would have been natural.

Ettingers Schuhwarenhaus
advertising stamp (circa 1910)

Salomon and Johanna lost all their business and their finances to the persecution of the Nazis in the 1930s. Likely due to sponsorship by Salomon's brother Arnold, in 1939 Salomon and Johanna were able to book passage on the RMS Queen Mary (sharing passage with pianist Vladimir Horowitz's wife Wanda, daughter of Arturo Toscanini, and their daughter Sophie).

In the US they joined their daughter Elisa (in the US she went as Alice) Ettinger, for whom my wife Jeanette Elisa would one day be named. Dr. Ettinger was a highly regarded professor at Tufts University who was one of the key people to launch modern gastrointestinal radiology in the US after her arrival from Berlin in 1932.

Also seen in the photo are Alice's sister Paula and Paula's husband Gerhard Roemer, parents of my source Michael Roemer. His parents divorced when he was a young child but managed to survive the war as well. Gerhard made his way to Spain in 1934 and later England and died there. His mother Paula stayed in Berlin and when the war began got work in a German munitions factory, where she was considered an excellent employee. Likely through her sister Alice's intercession from the US, she obtained a permit to leave Germany for Portugal and then the US in June 1941. Prior to that, in 1939, Paula had arranged for her eleven-year-old son Michael and eight-year-old daughter Marianne to be included in the Kindertransport, as one of nearly 10,000 predominantly Jewish children from Europe who were rescued from peril in Europe and placed in British foster living quarters. Michael later recalled that in the haste of departing Vienna, he did not have a photo of his mother to take with him. By the time the war ended and Michael emigrated to the US six years later in 1945, he had forgotten what she looked like. On landing in the US, he was only reunited with her at shipside when she recognized him.

The seventeen-year-old immigrant then enrolled as an undergraduate at Harvard University.

Max (11), Fella, and Edith Pollak (51): Max, whose wife Fella (née Leiser) was a maternal aunt of the bride, was Jeanette's great-grandfather. Their lineage began Chapter Five. Max specialized as a glove manufacturer within the Leiser family shoe enterprise. As noted above in the section about his wife's uncle Salomon, for a time he also owned the Ettinger Shoe Warehouse. When I look at the photo, informed by the knowledge that Max would die a decade later in 1936 of tuberculosis, I can only think of his relative good fortune of not having survived another seven years beyond then to share with his wife Fella (also called Fanny) her fate. Fella fled Germany on March 4, 1939 along with their daughter (and Jeanette's grandmother) Edith (née Pollak) Taubenschlag and Edith's husband and two children on a plane to Amsterdam to escape the Germans. Unlike Edith and her husband Heinz and their children Peter and Gabrielle, as described in the prior chapter, Fella was not able later to get a permit to leave Holland and was arrested by German forces there. Although Edith knew her mother did not survive the war, as late as 1981 she didn't know her exact fate. So when Edith filled out a page of testimony that August for the permanent record of the Yad Vashem Research Institute in Jerusalem, she could only leave the "Circumstances of Death" section blank. By 2011, the records of the International Tracing Service were available to me from the US Holocaust Memorial Museum in Washington. With their help, I could soon trace the records of Fella's arrest in Amsterdam on January 26, 1943 and later incarceration at the Vught concentration camp. From there she was sent to the Scheveningen police prison, and then on March 31, 1943, as her niece Lilo, she was sent to the Westerbork concentration camp. In her daughter Edith's

Polak-Huisman	Clara	26.12.12	den Haag,Zwetsstr.32	19.10.43
Polak	David	6.10. 64	" L.v.N.I.O. 143	19.10.43
Polak	David	6.7. 82	A,dam, A.Cuypstr.195	19.10.43
Polak	David	9.10. 95	" Ruyschstr.78 entl.10.8.43	
Polak-Nbarro	Dora	23.5. 99	" Dintelstr.38	19.10.43
Polak	Elisabeth	29.1. 35	den Haag,Zwetsstr.33	19.10.43
Polak-Leiser	Fanny	8.6. 84	A,dam, Krammerstr.1	19.10.43
Polak-Smalhout	Frederika	5.6. 98	" Polegstr.111	19.10.43
Polak	Gerard	8.4. 12	" Bouwermanstr.6 ent.6.9.43	
Polak-Cohen	Henriette	8.11. 56	" Pr.Hendrikkd-144 16.9.43 entl.	

Section from deportation records from Westerbork
to Auschwitz-Birkenau Death Camps

papers I recently found a copy of several letters that Fella wrote from the Westerbork camp between March and September to an attorney in Portugal desperately seeking help. All were in vain. The last record of her life appears on the paperwork documenting deportations from Westerbork to Auschwitz, noting the transport date of October 19, 1943. Her name appears midway down the page as "Polak-Leiser" alongside her birthdate, last address before her arrest, and date of transport.

Fella was sister to the bride's mother and her husband Max and daughter Edith were both in the wedding photo, so her absence from the photo surprised me. As with the non-photographed bride's sister Käthe above, Fella was also surely present at the wedding, as the *spiel* program lists her as playing the role of "*die heiratsvermittlerin*," the matchmaker. Fella, too, may well have been getting into costume as the photo was taken.

OTTO AND ELLA (NÉE SIEGER) KLAUSNER (16): Otto Klausner was six years junior to his brother Julius. I have not yet identified him as one of the men in the photo, but, as his wife Ella was identified by Lilo in the photo, I suspect he is also there. Otto was successful in his own right in the German shoe industry. Following a few years later in the footsteps of Julius, as an eighteen-year-old he founded the Otto Klausner

company as a wholesale business. In 1923 Otto entered shoe
retailing, founding the Bottina
Schuh company eventually having eighteen branches in North
and Central Germany. He died
at age fifty-one in 1931, shortly
before the Nazis rose to power in
Germany. As the German government forced Jewish ownership out, the eighteen branches
of the retail outlets were sold to
others at giveaway prices, and
Otto's widow Ella was given little
compensation. With the significant financial assistance of her
brother-in-law Julius Klausner

Otto Klausner shoes
advertising stamp, artist
Leo Prochownik (circa 1912)

in obtaining a passport, Ella later escaped Germany for the Netherlands but was arrested there after the German occupation. The Dutch
oorlogsgravenstichting.nl memorial database records her has having died
at the Sobibór Death Camp in occupied Poland on May 14, 1943. See
Frank Bajohr, *"Aryanisation" in Hamburg: The Economic Exclusion of Jews
and the Confiscation of their Property in Nazi Germany*. Translated by
George Wilke. (Monographs in German History, number 7.) New York:
Berghahn Books. 2002. Pp. vii, 344.

HARRY AND MARGARETHE (GRETHE) (NÉE SIEGER) HAUPTMANN (14):
Grete was the sister of Ella (née Sieger) Klausner (16). As with the interlocking relationships in full evidence at this wedding, Grethe was likely

in attendance not just as the sister of an aunt-of-the-bride by marriage. Her husband Harry, whom I do not think is in the photo, was, however, an intimate part of the day's festivities, as musical director of the *spiel* that accompanied the wedding mentioned earlier in the context of other relatives who were not in the photo. Harry was a famous songwriter in pre-war Berlin, so he would have been a natural accompaniment to the wedding party. He was best known for his song "Die Dame Mit Dem Monokel," (The Lady with the Monocle). Harry and Grethe escaped from Germany to spend the war years as part of the large refugee Jewish community in Shanghai, China. In 1947 they immigrated to the US.

SABINE (NÉE KLAUSNER) ETTINGER (22) AND ARNOLD ETTINGER: Amidst the Ettinger and Klausner and Leiser families of Tarnów, in-marriage was not unusual. One family member has said that some of the occasional eccentricity (see later in this section) in various branches of the family may have been a product of the inbreeding. It may have arisen from both the large size of the extended families, the recurrent interaction in common business and social affairs, and a possible desire to keep their wealth and business control within the family. One example was the marriage of Julius Klausner and his cousin Dora Leiser. Another was that of Julius's sister Sabine Klausner to her uncle Arnold Ettinger, only five years older than Sabine. Arnold was also in the shoe business and was the family's pioneer in the United States. Because he was living in Berlin in the 1920s, I suspect that he is also one of the still-unidentified men in the photo, but his wife Sabine certainly is in the photo.

Arnold was born in Tarnów in 1867 and traveled to the US at age seventeen and moved to South Carolina, where he learned American business methods and developed the connections, including obtaining American citizenship, that he would later expand on for a career of importing

American shoes to be sold back in Germany. Sabine gave birth to their three children in Berlin, where the family maintained their primary residence, though US census records show the family as having a residence in the US as well throughout the first decades of the twentieth century. Arnold died at age seventy-four in Alexandria, Virginia and Sabine lived till age ninety-one. The two are buried there as well. Their grandson Robert Chester Wilson Ettinger fought as an American artillery lieutenant and won a Purple Heart medal in the World War II Battle of the Bulge against the Germans. He achieved international attention as the father of the cryonics movement, having written the 1964 book "Prospect of Immortality." As much interested in his notoriety as his family connection, I had the pleasure of speaking with him when he was age ninety-one in a 2010 phone interview. He died the following year, and, to the best of my knowledge, his remains remain in frozen storage to this day, along with those of his mother and both his first and second wives.

Appendix 2

JEWISH GENEALOGICAL TOOLS

There are numerous sources for the do-it-yourself Jewish genealogist, and I'm pleased to share a few.

The core starting point is interviewing your own family. Find every living relative you can and ask them who they know about in the family tree. Search out your oldest relatives first and interview them. They will be gone before you know it, and the time to ask them questions is now. Make detailed notes, and, if they are willing, record their conversation. They may mention names and places that mean nothing to you today but may well be gold mines of information down the road.

Once you're beginning to acquire information, you will want to record it systematically. Be compulsive and record not just the information you obtain, but also the specific sources for each bit of information.

Having a detailed record of the sources will be of immense use down the road when you discover that you need to double-check one detail of which you are uncertain or when someone else asks you to establish the provenance of a genealogical record you've uncovered. We all make mistakes in recording data and having a solid trail back to your original source will help you correct those errors.

Systematic recording is most easily done with a software application. Some people use online crowd-sourced family trees such as MyHeritage.com or Geni.com. Others record their trees on Ancestry .com. My preference is using a Mac/PC-based application on my own computer. I am a Macintosh user and have been pleased with Reunion for Macintosh for decades. It has an extremely user-friendly interface and is great for capturing all forms of genealogical data and creating genealogical charts, reports, and books. Other applications that run on both PCs and Macs that have been well-reviewed are Family Tree Maker and Roots Magic. New and revised versions of these and other similar software packages are continually coming on the market. Whichever software solution one chooses, meticulous recording of your findings will make your genealogical life more accurate. The days of keeping your genealogical records on scraps of paper or index cards or file folders represent a glorious past more than a productive future. Having said that, for posterity I still do keep file folders for original documents and memorabilia and photos after I've scanned them into digital images.

The next critical software tool for Jewish genealogy is JewishGen .org. This website offers its immense database to the world at no charge for simple searches. Donors of $100 can access advanced search features. JewishGen also offers an interactive online Jewish genealogy course to teach methodology and research techniques. The website runs a "Family

Finder" that facilitates finding links to other people worldwide who might be researching your family. JewishGen's online discussion groups are a superb forum for asking specific questions about almost any Jewish genealogical topic.

Two Facebook groups, in particular, offer a worldwide scope for rapid feedback questions and answers: "Jewish Genealogy Portal" and "Tracing the Tribe—Jewish Genealogy on Facebook." Once you've looked at those Facebook groups, there are numerous specialized Facebook groups focusing on Jewish genealogy in particular regions of the world. (Disclosure: I moderate "Jewish Genealogy Poland" on Facebook.)

If you're looking for one book, Gary Mokotoff's *Getting Started in Jewish Genealogy 2018 Edition* is a perfect introduction. It gives special focus to two oft-stated and fixable challenges to uncovering Jewish genealogy: specifically, the myth that "the family name was changed at Ellis Island" and the lack of awareness of the town where one's ancestors came from in "the Old country." *Avotaynu*, the International Journal of Jewish Genealogy publishes four issues a year of its in-depth journal.

Ancestry.com is a great, if pricey, storehouse of resources for finding lost relatives. If you are not willing to pay their membership fee, perhaps your local public library subscribes to the website as a public service and you could use it at no cost there? I convinced my local library to take out a subscription! Other online databases such as Geni.com and MyHeritage.com can be extremely useful. As the data supplied to those crowd-sourced databases are not necessarily fact-checked for accuracy or documentation, it is worth taking the information available in those sources as starting points for research, but not as definitive until independently supported by documentary or other sources. People will often post suppositions or guesses or family legends of relationships, which are sometimes true and sometimes myth.

After one has been pursuing one's family tree for a year or two, one way to combine travel with genealogy research would be to attend an annual meeting of the International Association of Jewish Genealogical Societies (IAJGS). Typically held each year somewhere across the globe in summer, novices and experts have a lot of fun and learn an immense amount by attending the conference for a day or two. Often lecturers will deliver critical nuggets leading to a gold mine of genealogical information either in their talks, or in "curbside" consultations outside the formal talks. Exhibitors' booths often provide additional resources.

DNA testing is beyond the scope of this book and raises a host of privacy questions and concerns. There are certainly reports of people finding previously unknown (and sometimes unthinkable) relatives from DNA testing. In my own case, a daughter and I used one of the commercial DNA testing companies and did not learn substantially new information. While I found in my case that my DNA indicated 99.2 percent Ashkenazi Jewish background, and my daughter found biological evidence linking her to my wife's first cousins, these data were hardly a surprise. We were given the names of a few possible distant relatives, but so far have not been able either to confirm if we are, in fact, related to them or not. Nonetheless, the ubiquity of the advertising and the simplicity of salivary DNA testing suggests that this tool will continue to grow more popular, especially when one is probing more distant reaches of the family tree.

Endnotes

INTRODUCTION

1 William Shakespeare, *Romeo and Juliet*, act 2, scene 2, lines 1–2.
2 Tami Luhby, "Celebrating a father's spirit," *The Home News [New Brunswick, New Jersey]*, June 19, 1995, pp. B1, B4.

CHAPTER 1

1 As of this writing in 2018, the future of Jewish life in Poland is again being questioned by some in the wake of Poland's government enacting a new law threatening criminal penalties for the use of the imprecise term of "Polish Death Camps" and consideration of a new law barring export of kosher meat from Poland. Leading church and government officials continue to encourage a meaningful and strong future for Jewish life in Poland.
2 Shmuel Levin and Daniel Blatman, "מרקושוב," *Pinkas Hakehillot*, Encyclopaedia of Jewish Communities, POLAND, Vol. VII, editor Abraham Wein. Yad Vashem, Jerusalem, 1999, pp. 315–317.
3 David Silberklang, Gates of Tears: The Holocaust in the Lublin District. Yad Vashem, Jerusalem, 2013.

4   Most Jews did not have fixed surnames in this part of Poland until the early nine-teenth century. Having a surname, however, did not necessarily mean using it on a tombstone, however.

5   "אִם בָּאֲרָזִים נָפְלָה שַׁלְהֶבֶת, מַה יַּעֲשׂוּ אֵזוֹבֵי קִיר?" Mo'ed Katan, *Babylonian Tal-mud*. 25b:20.

6   As of this writing, the photos can be viewed at teatrnn.pl/ikonografia/negatywy/kategoria/10. A Polish language account of the discovery of the identity of the photographer is at http://teatrnn.pl/kalendarium/node/2079/autor_kolekcji_szklanych_negatyw%C3%B3w_z_rynku_4_odnaleziony.

7   As of this writing, the photo can be viewed at teatrnn.pl/ikonografia/negatywy/zdjecie/2499#negatywy_zdjecie_etykieta.

8   Prov. 31:10–31.

9   1 Sam. 25:29.

10 Rabbi Gil Nativ, Ph.D., helped me see the rhyming scheme that makes the epi-taph a form of poetry. The first and third lines end with a "reem" sound from the Hebrew letters Resh-Yud-Memsofit (רִים). The second and fourth lines end with a "mayeem" sound from the Hebrew letters Mem-Yud-Memsofit (מַיִם). The fifth and seventh lines end with an "anu" sound from the Hebrew letters Nun-Vav (נוּ). The sixth and eighth lines end with an "orot" sound from the Hebrew let-ters Vav-Resh-Vav-Taf (וֹרוֹת). The ninth and tenth lines recapitulate the original rhyme ending with an "omeem" sound from the Hebrew letters Vav-Mem-Yud-Memsofit (וּמִים). Together the poetry rhyme fits an ABAB CDCD EE pattern.

11 Zeev Kainan has suggested that the first word could be read as שְׁאָו and therefore could be echoing the concept of calamity in the Hebrew word of shoah (שׁוֹאָה) originally derived from Isaiah 47:11. By that reading the line could be translated into English as, *"Listen to us and we shall weep bitterly."*

12 Lam. 2: 18.

13 Rabbi Nativ observed that this Hebrew language mirrors that of Joel 2:10, which describes the overwhelming fear and depression to be associated with an upcoming day of judgment. Rabbi Baumol found that this reference to constel-lations (מזרות) and the verb of being collected or taken away (נאסף) mirrors the biblical texts of Job 38:32 and Isaiah 57:1, respectively, in which the Bible discusses the inexplicability of the premature death of righteous or beloved people.

14 The acronym ה'ה' (hey-hey) is either an honorific abbreviation for הרי היא—"she is" or for הלא היא—"indeed, it is."

15 Prov. 10:7.

16 Experts who have seen this text have not reported knowing of such liberties taken on other tombstones. Zeev Kainan has suggested that the extra hey (ה) could be an abbreviation for the Hebrew word for he (הוא), so referring to her father.

17 By some approaches to calculating *g'matriya*, *Dalet* equals the number 4, *Lamed* equals the number 30, and *Chafsofit* equals 500. The three letters together represent the sum, or 534. By Jewish convention, in writing a year using Hebrew letters, 5000 is added to that total, meaning the Jewish year represented by *Dalet Lamed Chafsofit* would be 5534.

18 During many of the years that the area of Poland in which Markuszów was under Russian control, civil records were recorded in the Russian language.

19 Hebcal.com notes this is the week for reading this *Torah* portion in the "diaspora"—countries outside of Israel where Jews have lived.

20 Rabbi Gil Nativ pointed out that the renowned biblical commentator Rashi (Rabbi Shlomo Yitzchaki) had observed, in his commentary on the Genesis 1:14 story of creation of the lights in the sky, that Wednesday was considered in the Talmudic era to be a "cursed" day of the week, because it was associated with children becoming ill with croup. Rashi noted that the word for "luminaries" in the heavens, if it were spelled as a homonym "מְאוֹרֹת," can also be read as a pun on curses "מְאֵרֹת." This adds further to the sense of the family that Sarah Chana's death on that Wednesday made it a truly terrible day.

CHAPTER 2

1 I thank Meyer Denn for taking photos of the mosaics.

2 Nechama Tec, Doba-Necha Cukierman, and Ida Gliksztejn published reports and specific examples of thefts, threats and hostility and a number of violent and life-threatening incidents by non-Jews toward Jews in postwar Lublin that contributed to the general feeling of Jews that it was unsafe for them to stay in Lublin or to try to reclaim their former property. See the Epilogue in Nechama Tec, *Dry Tears: The Story of a Lost Childhood*. New York: Oxford University Press. 1984. Also see Doba-Necha Cukierman, *A Guardian Angel: Memories of Lublin*. Editor: Ester Csaky. East Bentleigh, Australia: Ester Csaky. 1997. Also see Ida Gliksztejn, *A Memoir from the War*. Lublin, Poland: Grodzka Gate Theater NN Center. 2017. Reports such as this abound from postwar Poland. For example, Morry Chandler (formerly Moszek Tuchendler) described a painful example of postwar neighbors' actions in the Polish town of Nasielsk. Returning to his hometown after pretending to be a Catholic during the war, he found the hidden storeroom in his murdered family's former home where his family and many neighbors had previously hidden their personal treasures in the hope of recovering them after the war. Together with another Jew and some local Polish assistants they broke the seal to the space. Moments afterwards "the whole town," he reported, came rushing in to the space and plundered all the objects in the room. For his own safety, Chandler did not identify himself as *de jure* owner of the home and property and walked away empty-handed. The memory was indelible and one of many that created a poisoned legacy for Poland in the eyes of

Jewish survivors. See Glenn Kurtz, *Three Minutes in Poland: Discovering a Lost World in a 1938 Family Film*. New York: Farrar, Straus, and Giroux. 2014. Also see, *The Jews in Poland Since the Liberation*, US Department of State Intelligence Research Report OCL-2312, May 15, 1946. Also see, Peter Sedgman, *As Far as I Can See*. Sydney, Australia: Sydney Jewish Museum. 2006, p. 38.

3   See Shimshon Leib Kirshenboim et al. "Lublin." *Encyclopaedia Judaica*, edited by Michael Berenbaum and Fred Skolnik, 2nd ed., vol. 13, Macmillan Reference US, Farmington Hills, Michigan. 2007, pp. 242–245.

4   This illustration is adapted from *Atlas Historii Żydów Polskich*, maps by Witold Sienkiewicz, Demart, Warsaw, 2010, p. 344.

5   *The United States Holocaust Memorial Museum Encyclopedia of CAMPS AND GHETTOS, 1933–1945, Vol. II, Part A*, edited by Martin Dean, Indiana University Press, Bloomington, 2012, pp. 607, 675.

6   See references to Siedliszcze in David Silberklang, *Gates of Tears: The Holocaust in the Lublin District*. Jerusalem: Yad Vashem. 2013. Also see the history of Siedliszcze in the Virtual Sztetl websiste.

7   Modern land records still record other murdered Gewerces and their descendants as partial inheritors of the property. I thank Tadeusz Przystojecki and his associate Ziemowit Karłowicz for their painstaking work to investigate the ownership history of 7 Grodzka.

CHAPTER 3

1   To date I have not been able to find a copy of her birth certificate. Her marriage certificate records her given name as Freda, though her name was certainly pronounced as if "Frieda" was the correct spelling.

2   Philip Roth, "The Last Days of Herman Roth," an adapted excerpt from *Patrimony*, published in *The New York Times Magazine*, Dec. 30, 1990, pp. 17–22.

3   Philip Roth, *The Facts: A Novelist's Autobiography*. Vintage Books, New York, 1988.

4   Charles McGrath, "Philip Roth, Towering Novelist Who Explored Lust, Jewish Life and America, Dies at 85," *The New York Times*, May 24, 2018, pp. A28–A29.

5   Eric Cortellessa, "The story behind Philip Roth's final days," *The Times of Israel*, May 25, 2018.

CHAPTER 4

1   The original film (and a digital copy of it) was since donated by Gaby to become part of the collection the Jewish Museum of Berlin.

2   As this book went to press, I discovered (based in significant part on the work of Randol Schoenberg on geni.com) that Karoline, a daughter of David Loew Schlosser, is a direct descendant of sixteenth century Rabbi Yehuda ben Betzalel

Loew, known as the "Maharal of Prague." Though the Maharal is an illustrious ancestor of my wife's, this knowledge is tempered by the likelihood that there are thousands of people alive today who are also his descendants: most having no such awareness of that history.

3   In later years I would find in old family records a surviving 1929 letter written by Ludwig from Rome to his brother Max in Berlin further confirming that the famous Ludwig was in fact our Max's brother. See Margarete Merkel Guldan, *Die Tagebucher Von Ludwig Pollak: Kennerschaft und Kunsthandel in Rom (1893-1943)*, Des Historischen Instituts Beim Österreichischen Kulturinstitut in Rom, Verlag Der Österriechischen Akademie der Wissenschaften, Vienna, 1988.

4   Lynn Catterson, "Michelangelo's 'Laocoön?,'" *Artibus et Historiae*, 2005, vol. 26, pp. 29–56.

5   Transferred from his home after his deportation, Pollak's personal archive is today in the possession of the reconstituted Museo di Scultura Antica Giovanni Barracco in Rome. (I thank Maddalena Cima, director of the Museo Barracco for her 2010 correspondence on this matter.)

6   https://www.archives.gov/iwg/declassified-records/rg-239-monuments-salvage -commission/

7   If, as Moltesen has suggested, conversion had been a requirement for sanctuary in the Vatican, Pollak might indeed have asked himself whether he was being asked to pay an unthinkable existential price for the lives of himself and his family. A clue to his own inner feelings about his Jewish background comes from Pollak's characterization of the Russian-Jewish painter Yehuda Epstein in which Pollak writes about Epstein that "especially sympathetic in him was his never denied devotion to his people." Guldan, herself, however, never found any evidence that conversion was discussed as a requirement for sanctuary in the Vatican. Mette Moltesen, "Review of *Ludwig Pollak, Römische Memoiren: Künstler, Kunstliebhaber und Gelehrte 1893-1943*, ed. Margarete Merkel Guldan. Rome, L'Erma di Bretschneider, 1994," in *Journal of the History of Collections*, 1996, vol. 8, pp. 221-222; e-mail from Margarete Merkel Guldan to author, August 20, 2016.

8   William Faulkner, *Requiem for a Nun*, Random House, New York, 1951.

9   The Museum of Palazzo Venezia in Rome also received many other gifts from Nicod from the collections of Pollak that had been saved from the Nazi raids.

CHAPTER 5

1   Margot Klausner, *Julius Klausner—Eine Biographie*. Kalima-Druck, Düsseldorf, 1974.

2   Some of this history was aided immensely by conversations with Mooly Landesman (great-granddaughter of Julius and Dora Klausner), and historical information and photos from the US Holocaust Memorial Museum and by the writings

of and conversations with Darlene Julia Shely (named after Julius Klausner), granddaughter of Josef Leiser.

3 Mooly Landesman kindly provided to me copies of the receipts and legal documents associated with these exit payments. Julius and Dora paid 1,364,652 Reichsmarks (RM) as *Reichsfluchtsteuer* (exit tax) and 2,250,000 RM for their passports.

4 I thank Mooly Landesman for calling my attention to the relevant sections of her grandmother's biography of Julius Klausner, cited above.

5 See the extensive records documenting Rautenberg's postwar arrests for smuggling "millions" worth of contraband jewelry from Holland shortly after the war as recorded in publication M1926, Records of the Reparations and Restitutions Branch of the US Allied Commission for Austria (USACA) Section, 1945-1950, in the United States National Archives, roll 0027, file 141. This section was also aided by an online article about Lilo's family's interaction with the Grimoldis: clarin.com/sociedad/AMIA-destacan-solidaridad-Grimoldi -victimas_0_986901361.html, published September 4, 2013, shortly before Lilo's death.

6 This section was especially aided by the writings of Darlene Shely published in the June 2007 and June 2008 issues of the Berlin publication *aktuell*. I am grateful to Darlene and her mother Josefine Leiser for sharing with me their recollections.

7 *The New York Times*, March 13, 1964, page 33.

8 Business aspects of Del-Ka are described in Gerald D. Feldman's comprehensive *Austrian Banks in the Period of National Socialism*, German Historical Institute, Washington, DC, 2015, especially pages 8, 18, and 265–281.

9 See, for example, Avraham Barkai and Paul Mendes-Flohr, "Exclusion and Persecution: 1933-1938," in *German-Jewish History in Modern Times*, vol. 4, ed. Michael A. Meyer, Columbia University Press, 1996, pages 216–217.

10 G.E.R. Gedye, "Nazis List 1,742 Jailed in Austria," *The New York Times*, March 23, 1938, p. 8.

11 Klausner's cellmate Bruno Heilig, an Austrian journalist also arrested and sent to Dachau published his recollections of Klausner's words and the Dachau 1938 conditions in *Men Crucified*, Eyre & Spottiswood, 1941. See also Kim Wünschmann, *Before Auschwitz: Jewish Prisoners in the Prewar Concentration Camps*, Harvard University Press, 2015.

12 The April 1, 1938 Gestapo deportation list and Dachau registration records identifying him may be found at http://www.doew.at/erinnern/fotos-und -dokumente/1938-1945/der-erste-dachau-transport-aus-wien-1-april-1938. Additional source material about Dachau, the "Prominentransport," and Buchenwald can be found in Giles MacDonogh, *1938: Hitler's Gamble*, Basic Books, New York, 2009 and in Wolfgang Neugebauer's essay in Maximilian and Emilie

Reich, *Two Witnesses' Testimony*, Francis Michael Sharp translation, Ariadne Press, Riverside, California, 2013. I am grateful to William Connelly at the US Holocaust Memorial Museum for referring me to the International Tracing Service records of Ludwig Klausner from Dachau and Buchenwald.

13 See Feldman, page 265. Also see section 4.4 in the Nook e-book by Norman Goda: *The Holocaust: Europe, the World, and the Jews, 1918–1945*.

14 See, for example, *The New York Times* of May 7, 1938, "New Suicide Wave Breaks Out in Vienna," p. 5, and June 28, 1938, "Wave of Suicides Renewed in Vienna.," p. 7. I thank Traude Triebel for her work in collecting names of people known to have committed suicide in Vienna in 1938.

CHAPTER 6

1 I thank US Holocaust Memorial Museum volunteer Peter Lande and researcher Steven Vitto for tracking down some of the records of Käthe's final years.

2 Though Iris would one day come to doubt whether this was true, or even whether the man who claimed to be her grandfather was really her grandfather, a family letter I recently found among Jeanette's grandmother's papers from 1981 confirms that Heinrich's nephew Hans in fact had visited Heinrich in Sao Paolo at some point after the war.

3 Just before the Battle of Arnhem in September, 1944, Kees, Geert, and little Iris evacuated the city by bicycling approximately 75 miles (120 km) to Zaandam, where Kees's father lived.

4 I thank Iris for hosting Jeanette and me for an afternoon with all three of her children in her Netherlands home in 2018 and for her and son Niels offering very helpful edits in the preparation of this chapter. Any errors are my own.

CHAPTER 7

1 At the time of this writing, Mirsky is a rabbinical student at the University of Judaism in Los Angeles, California.

2 To help address the immense need for resources, in 2016 I and a group of American colleagues founded an IRS-approved non-profit 501(c)(3) organization called the "Friends of Jewish Heritage in Poland." We provide an easy conduit for donations to support the work of restoration of Jewish cemeteries and synagogues in Poland and we invite people to contribute to the care of the sites in the locations of interest to their own ancestry, or to support the work in general. For more information see jewishheritagepoland.org.

3 I was introduced this group of modern-day saints and their leader Steven D. Reece by Monika Krawczyk, executive director of FODŻ, and her social-media savvy associate Marla Raucher Osborn. When I knew that I wanted to find a way to clean up the Markuszów cemetery I reached out to Monika, whose FODŻ organization was the legal owner of the cemetery, and to Marla, an American

FODŹ staff member at the time who was working hard to build partnerships for FODŹ with descendants of Polish Jewish communities.

4 See for example, Anna Bikont, *The Crime and the Silence*, Farrar, Straus, and Giroux, New York, 2004, 2015 translation by Alissa Valles.

5 Ta'anit, *Babylonian Talmud*, 2a.

6 In 2016 he would secure a half-million Euro grant from the European Union to support his work in restoring that Jewish cemetery.

CHAPTER 8

1 *Mishnah Sanhedrin.* 4.5.

2 Kaja Finkler, Professor Emeritus of Anthroplogy at the University of North Carolina is my fourth cousin once removed on my maternal grandfather's side. Through happenstance I only learned of her within the year before finishing this book and just met her in person even more recently. Her poignant narrative of her and her mother's survival of the Shoah is recounted in Kaja Finkler and Golda Finkler, *Lives Lived and Lost*, Academic Studies Press, Brighton, Massachusetts, 2012.

Photo Credits

All family tree diagrams were produced by Dan Oren and Jeanette Kuvin Oren

Chapter 7

Appendix I

Acknowledgments

In text and footnotes along the way, I have tried to mention key people who have made this journey possible, hoping that in my human imperfection, I have not forgotten to mention too many. In this closing space, I need to recognize a few people whose contributions were particularly broad.

The book would never have happened without my late mother Rebeka Oren taking me on my first trip to find our roots in Poland back in 1993 and my late father Gideon Oren, in poor health at that time yielding to my encouragement to going without my mother's support during the week of that trip. I am only sorry they are not alive to see these results. But I have no doubt they would find meaning in the rescue of our history. To Markuszów cemetery historian

Paweł Sygowski and Matzevah Foundation president Steven Reece, I am always in debt for helping physically and psychologically to find the hidden history that lay in that cemetery. Tomasz Pietrasiewicz and his wonderful staff at the Grodzka Gate living museum in Lublin helped me find the lost history of my great-grandmother and the house she lived in, and, even more importantly, serve as a fountain of hope reinforcing the value of rediscovering and teaching history. Mooly Landesman's unhesitating sharing with me of "The Wedding Photo" opened a broad and deep portal into the past of not just her grandmother's wedding, but also my wife Jeanette's entire maternal history. Precious Skype conversations with the late Lilo (Liselotte) Leiser Nesviginsky were a living entry to a lost family from almost a century ago. Without her the people in the wedding photo would have been mostly a collection of strangers. Joan Kuvin Olsson generously shared with me the remarkable story of her discovery of her ancestry and partnered with me in probing it more completely. Dr. Michael Nevins and David Sanford Cohen generously shared with me their knowledge of the Chuwen/Cohen and Roth families. Margarete Merkel Guldan, whose dissertation unlocked the hidden diaries of Ludwig Pollak, was generous in sharing with me the details of her groundbreaking studies of Pollak. Iris van Popta-Dubbink graciously shared the personal details of her seemingly miraculous survival in childhood. David B. Green, fourth cousin-once-removed Kaja Finkler, Sydney Perry, and Amalyah Oren all read early drafts of this book and provided critical counsel. Laura Morton shared with me her vital wisdom about the publishing world, including introducing me to Meghan Day Healey, whose design talents show through on every page. All typos and mistakes in the book remain my own.

To my wife Jeanette Kuvin Oren (who spent countless hours drafting family trees and meeting innumerable new relatives) and my children Sarah and Amalyah, who also came to take interest in this hobby, I am ever grateful for the fullness of family that you have shared.

www.ingramcontent.com/pod-product-compliance
Lightning Source LLC
Chambersburg PA
CBHW040931030426

42334CB00007B/110